Dirtmeister's
Nitty Gritty
PLANET EARTH

DIRTMEISTER'S Nitty Gritty PLANET EARTH

ALL ABOUT ROCKS, MINERALS, FOSSILS, EARTHQUAKES, VOLCANOES, & EVEN DIRT!

Steve Tomecek
aka The Dirtmeister®

Illustrated by Fred Harper

NATIONAL GEOGRAPHIC KiDS

WASHINGTON, D.C.

Staff for this book
Erica Green, *Senior Editor*
Julide Dengel, *Art Director and Designer*
Lisa Jewell, *Photo Editor*
Paige Towler, *Editorial Assistant*
Sanjida Rashid, *Design Production Assistant*
Michael Cassady, *Photo Assistant*
Grace Hill, *Managing Editor*
Joan Gossett, *Senior Production Editor*
Lewis R. Bassford, *Production Manager*
Nicole Elliott, *Manager, Production Services*
Susan Borke, *Legal and Business Affairs*

Published by the National Geographic Society
Gary E. Knell, *President and CEO*
John M. Fahey, *Chairman of the Board*
Melina Gerosa Bellows, *Chief Education Officer*
Declan Moore, *Chief Media Officer*
Hector Sierra, *Senior Vice President and General Manager, Book Division*

Senior Management Team, Kids Publishing and Media
Nancy Laties Feresten, *Senior Vice President;* Jennifer Emmett, *Vice President, Editorial Director, Kids Books;* Julie Vosburgh Agnone, *Vice President, Editorial Operations;* Rachel Buchholz, *Editor and Vice President,* NG Kids *magazine;* Michelle Sullivan, *Vice President, Kids Digital;* Eva Absher-Schantz, *Design Director;* Jay Sumner, *Photo Director;* Hannah August, *Marketing Director;* R. Gary Colbert, *Production Director*

Digital
Anne McCormack, *Director;* Laura Goertzel, Sara Zeglin, *Producers;* Jed Winer, *Special Projects Assistant;* Emma Rigney, *Creative Producer;* Brian Ford, *Video Producer;* Bianca Bowman, *Assistant Producer;* Natalie Jones, *Senior Product Manager*

The National Geographic Society is one of the world's largest nonprofit scientific and educational organizations. Founded in 1888 to "increase and diffuse geographic knowledge," the Society's mission is to inspire people to care about the planet. It reaches more than 400 million people worldwide each month through its official journal, *National Geographic,* and other magazines; National Geographic Channel; television documentaries; music; radio; films; books; DVDs; maps; exhibitions; live events; school publishing programs; interactive media; and merchandise. National Geographic has funded more than 10,000 scientific research, conservation, and exploration projects and supports an education program promoting geographic literacy.

For more information, please visit nationalgeographic.com, call 1-800-NGS LINE (647-5463), or write to the following address:

National Geographic Society
1145 17th Street N.W.
Washington, D.C. 20036-4688 U.S.A.

Visit us online at nationalgeographic.com/books

For librarians and teachers: ngchildrensbooks.org

More for kids from National Geographic:
kids.nationalgeographic.com

For information about special discounts for bulk purchases, please contact National Geographic Books Special Sales: ngspecsales@ngs.org

For rights or permissions inquiries, please contact National Geographic Books Subsidiary Rights: ngbookrights@ngs.org

Library of Congress Cataloging-in-Publication Data

Tomecek, Steve, author.
Dirtmeister's nitty gritty planet Earth : all about rocks, minerals, fossils, earthquakes, volcanoes, and even dirt! / by Steve Tomecek.
    p.   cm.
Includes bibliographical references and index.
Audience: 8-12.
ISBN 978-1-4263-1904-4 (reinforced library binding : alk. paper) — ISBN 978-1-4263-1903-7 (pbk. : alk. paper)
1. Geology—Juvenile literature. I. Title.
  QE29.T66 2015
  551—dc23
                                2014035353

Printed in Hong Kong
15/THK/1

Thanks to my good friend Jim "The Rockhound" Lucarelli for fact-checking the manuscript. To all my colleagues who survived the 1978 QUEENS COLLEGE GEOLOGY FIELD CAMP, especially my roommate ROB, my field partner MARSHALL, and DR. ALAN LUDMAN. You guys ROCK!

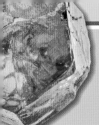

TABLE OF CONTENTS

> OH SORRY, DIDN'T SEE YOU THERE.

> NOT NOW, DIGGER, I'M TRYING TO WORK!

ALLOW ME TO INTRODUCE MYSELF. MY FRIENDS CALL ME "THE DIRTMEISTER."

Dirtmeister is a nickname that I picked up a long time ago because of the type of work that I do. You see, I'm a geologist, which means that I spend a lot of my time digging in the dirt. Geologists are scientists who study the Earth and try to understand how it got here and how it changes. We try to answer questions such as how different rocks form, why earthquakes happen, what causes volcanoes to erupt, and where fossils come from. Over the years I've gotten to do some pretty cool stuff as a scientist. I've also spent a lot of time working in radio and television and I've been on lots of websites. These days, my favorite thing to do is to hang out with kids and try to answer some of their questions about science and how the world works.

That's why I've put this book together. Over the years I've found that kids have lots of questions about how the Earth works, so I've gathered up the best of them and put them here. I've also come up with lots of cool facts called "Dirtmeister's Nuggets" and a few stories about the men and women who had a big influence in the field of geology. Inside this book, you'll find a bunch of experiments that you can do at home. You see, I'm not like some of those other scientists who say "don't do this at home." For me, science IS NOT a spectator sport. If you want to learn about how things work then you've got to mess around with stuff! Of course, before you start doing the experiments PLEASE grab an adult to help. That way if anything goes wrong you can blame them!

I guess the best way to think of me is as your tour guide to the inner workings of planet Earth. Along with my pal Digger, we'll "dig into" the Earth's past, see what makes our world tick, and even take a look at where we may be headed in the future. So put on your hard hat and climb aboard for a wild ride as we get the inside scoop on the planet we call home!

PULLING IT ALL TOGETHER

How does a humongous nebula turn into our wonderful rocky Earth? Scientists think that the gas and dust particles in the nebula were spread really far apart but gravity started pulling them closer together. Well, it turns out that everything that is made of matter (you know, stuff) has some gravity. The more massive an object is, the more gravitational pull it has.

All these tiny dust and gas particles started joining together to make bigger clumps. Over time, the nebula got smaller and started to spin. This spinning caused the nebula to flatten out to form a large disc. As the moving clumps of particles banged into each other they made bigger clumps.

Most of the stuff collected in the middle of the disc and this large clump became the sun. The smaller clumps became the planets and moons that we have today. The four planets closest to the sun—Mercury, Venus, Earth, and Mars—had lots of heavy materials such as iron and rock. The four outer planets—Jupiter, Saturn, Uranus, and Neptune—were more distant from the sun, where the pull of gravity was less, so they were made of lighter materials such as gases and ice.

Why do scientists think that a rotating disc of gas became the solar system? First off, all of the planets travel around the sun in the same direction and in the same basic plane. A plane is another name for a flat surface. If you were to look at our solar system edge on, the planets would all pretty much line up as if they were stretched across a giant tabletop. In addition, the sun is also on this same plane and it spins in the same direction that the planets move.

> A nebula is a large cloud of gas and dust.

A family portrait of the sun and the eight major planets of the solar system (not to scale)

A telescopic view of the Rosette Nebula

WHAT THE SOLAR SYSTEM MAY HAVE LOOKED LIKE WHEN THE EARTH WAS FIRST PULLING ITSELF TOGETHER

A close-up view of a typical asteroid

READY, AIM, ASTEROID BALL!

11

THE AGE IS ALL THE RAGE

OK, so how do scientists know how old the Earth is?

Well, to figure this out, we first have to understand what we call relative age. **Relative age** tells you if one thing is older than another but it doesn't tell you how old the different things are. For example, I can tell you that you are younger than your parents because they had to be born before you were. Your parents, on the other hand, are younger than your grandparents. So based on relative age your grandparents came first, then your parents, and then you.

Relative age is great for putting things in order, but it won't tell me exactly how old you or your parents are. In order to figure out your true ages, I would need to know the day, month, and year your grandparents, parents, and you were born. When we get an actual number for how old something is, we're talking about its **absolute age**.

Unfortunately, the rocks on the Earth do not come with birth certificates. At first, the best that early geologists could do was to come up with the relative ages of rocks. That gives me an idea for a little experiment.

> Scientists used relative and absolute age to calculate the age of the Earth.

TRY THIS! LAYERS OF TIME

WHAT YOU'LL NEED

A tall clear plastic cup
A box of raisins

A container of yogurt
A box of your favorite breakfast cereal

WHAT YOU'LL DO

Begin by pouring some of the raisins into the bottom of the cup. Make sure that there is a nice thick layer. Use the spoon to gently pour the yogurt on top of the raisins. Do NOT mix them together. Finally, sprinkle a layer of breakfast cereal on top of the yogurt.

Look at the cup from the side and you'll see that you have three distinct layers in the cup. So which came first? That's easy, the raisins. You know this because you were the one who poured them into the cup.

Suppose you didn't see the foods go into the cup. Do you think that you could still figure it out? Sure! You know from your own experiences that the layer of raisins on the bottom had to be there first, before the yogurt came on top. Since the cereal is on top of the yogurt, it had to be the last layer to go into the cup.

As your reward for being such an observant scientist you may now eat your experiment. (You may want to stir it up with a spoon first because it usually tastes better when mixed!)

A VIEW OF OUR EARTH FROM SPACE... SAY HI TO MOM!

HEY, DIGGER, YOU CAN'T STOP GEOLOGIC TIME!

DIRTMEISTER'S NUGGET

WHEN MOST PEOPLE THINK ABOUT TIME, THEY USUALLY THINK IN TERMS OF **HOURS, DAYS, MONTHS,** AND YEARS. THAT'S BECAUSE MOST PEOPLE NEVER LIVE TO BE OLDER THAN **100 YEARS OLD.** WHEN WE TALK ABOUT THE EARTH, 100 YEARS IS NOTHING! TO **MEASURE** THE AGE OF THE EARTH, SCIENTISTS USE SOMETHING CALLED **GEOLOGIC TIME,** WHICH COVERS **BILLIONS OF YEARS.** BASED ON THE LATEST MEASUREMENTS, MOST GEOLOGISTS AGREE THE **AGE OF THE EARTH** IS ABOUT **4,600,000,000 YEARS.**

IT'S ALL RELATIVE

OK, so you know how you just looked into your cup of yogurt to see what food went in first? Well, back in the mid-1600s, a Danish geologist named Nicolaus Steno made similar observations, except he did it with dirt! Steno watched how sand and clay formed layers as they filled up lakes and ponds. Since many rocks form with one layer on top of another, he came to the conclusion that if the rocks have not been moved, then the layer on the bottom would be the oldest and the layer on the top would be the youngest. This idea is called **superposition,** and it is used by geologists all over the world when they figure out the **relative age** of rocks.

About 100 years after Steno did his work, a Scottish scientist named James Hutton took it a few steps further. He realized that if one rock had pieces of another rock in it, then the second rock had to have been created before the first rock. That meant the second rock was older. Hutton spent a great deal of time making observations of the rocks found near his farm. Many of these were made up of layers of **sediment** that had become hardened over time. Hutton watched as layers of sediment filled in a lake near his home. He went back to the same place again and again and measured how long it took for the layers to build up. He found that it would take years for just a few inches of sediment to collect in the lake. When he looked around him he saw that some of the sediment layers in the rocks were hundreds of feet thick! There was no way that so much sediment could build up if the Earth was only a few thousand years old.

> "Sediment" is a word that geologists use to describe small particles of broken rock such as sand, pebbles, silt, and clay.

BIO JAMES HUTTON Uniformitarianism

BIRTHPLACE: SCOTLAND   BIRTH YEAR: 1726

Hutton believed that the Earth was changing all the time, but the rate of change was so slow that it was hard for people to see it. He said that given enough time, these slow and steady changes could completely reshape the Earth. At first his idea was not accepted but eventually other scientists came around to his way of thinking. Geologists now call his idea **uniformitarianism.**

Most often uniformitarianism can be explained by the phrase, "the present is the key to the past," which means that all the past changes that have happened to the Earth can be explained by processes that are happening on our Earth right now. Today, uniformitarianism is one of the most important concepts that we use when trying to figure out how the Earth has changed over time.

GEOLOGISTS USE SUPERPOSITION TO WORK OUT THE RELATIVE AGE OF LAYERED ROCKS.

BEFORE JAMES HUTTON, MOST OF THE PEOPLE WHO STUDIED THE EARTH BELIEVED THAT THE PLANET WAS ONLY ABOUT **6,000** YEARS OLD. THIS NUMBER WAS BASED ON THE WORK OF **RELIGIOUS SCHOLARS** WHO TRIED TO COME UP WITH AN AGE OF THE EARTH **BASED ON THE STORIES IN THE BIBLE.** IN THE MID-1600s **JAMES USSHER,** THE ARCHBISHOP OF IRELAND, EVEN CAME UP WITH AN **EXACT DATE FOR THE CREATION OF THE EARTH:** OCTOBER 23, 4004 B.C. AS IT TURNS OUT, SCIENTISTS BELIEVE HE WAS OFF BY A WEE BIT.

4004 BC.

I THINK WE NEED TO ADD SOME ZEROS TO THAT BIRTHDAY.

6000 y.o.

TIME MARCHES ON

By the mid-1800s many scientists were working on coming up with the **true age** of the Earth. One of the earlier scientists to work on this was Lord Kelvin. He believed that when the Earth first formed, it would have been a big ball of hot liquid rock called magma. He figured that the magma near the surface would cool first and turn into solid rock but the magma below the surface would remain melted. He based this idea on the fact that hot liquid magma can be seen coming up from below the surface in volcanoes today. By estimating how much rock had cooled on the planet's surface he came up with an age of the Earth of about 40 million years.

A few years later, in 1899, another British scientist named John Joly came up with a different idea. Joly knew that the reason ocean water is salty is that streams and rivers, which flow into oceans, have little particles of dissolved mineral salts in them. Joly said that all the water in the oceans started out as fresh water too and over time the salt slowly built up. By measuring the amount of salt found in freshwater streams and comparing it with the amount of salt found in ocean water, Joly came up with an even older age than Lord Kelvin did. He believed that the Earth was about 90 million years old.

Well, as you might imagine, there were a lot of arguments going on between scientists and it was hard to know who to believe. Thankfully, a real breakthrough came in 1896 when French scientist Henri Becquerel discovered that some rocks gave off an unusual type of energy. He didn't quite know what to make of it. But two years later, the husband and wife team of Marie and Pierre Curie unlocked the secret. They came up with a name for what Becquerel discovered. They called it **radioactivity.**

> Magma is hot liquid rock found inside the Earth.

URANINITE: EVEN THOUGH THIS PITCHBLENDE LOOKS HARMLESS, IT IS VERY DANGEROUS AND HIGHLY RADIOACTIVE.

MOST SCIENTISTS TODAY AGREE WITH LORD KELVIN THAT EARLY IN EARTH'S HISTORY, THE PLANET WAS MADE OF HOT MAGMA, AS SHOWN IN THIS ILLUSTRATION. THE MAGMA SLOWLY COOLED TO FORM THE SOLID EARTH.

BIO MARIE CURIE Radioactivity

BIRTHPLACE: POLAND   BIRTH YEAR: 1867

Marie Curie lived at a time when few women were allowed to work in science. Even though she was one of the top students in her school, she could not attend the University of Warsaw because it was for men only. Not giving up, Marie moved to France to earn her degree.

In 1903, Curie became the first woman to win a Nobel Prize—for her discovery of radioactivity—which she shared with her husband Pierre and Henri Becquerel.

During her research, she also discovered two new radioactive elements, radium and polonium, for which she won her second Nobel Prize in 1911.

Even though she was not a geologist, her work helped create a tool that would figure out how old the Earth was, and her discoveries helped other women have careers in science.

CLOCKS IN THE ROCKS

Marie and Pierre Curie were really good scientists, but at first even they couldn't understand what caused the radioactivity in the rocks. Another scientist, Ernest Rutherford, helped figure this out. In the early 1900s, scientists had already figured out that chemical elements could be broken down into tiny particles called atoms. Rutherford found that over time some atoms changed.

These special atoms started out as one chemical element and then slowly changed to a different, lighter element, releasing energy as they transformed. This process is called radioactive decay and it would be the thing that geologists could use to measure an absolute age of the Earth. That's when an American scientist named Bertram Borden Boltwood got into the age dating act. Back in 1907, he discovered a way to use this radioactive decay to measure how old certain rock types were.

When Boltwood first began conducting his experiments, things didn't go as planned. In fact, he thought that he had made some really serious errors because the ages he was getting were way off the chart. The first rock he tested produced an age of over 500 million years and the second was over 2 billion years old! These ages were way too old based on the ages that Lord Kelvin and John Joly had calculated. Boltwood checked over all his equipment and even retested the samples, but he could not find anything wrong. He began testing other rocks that he knew were younger, and those ages were correct. He could find no errors. Earth wasn't millions of years old—it was billions of years old!

> An atom is the smallest piece of a chemical element that still has all the properties of that element.

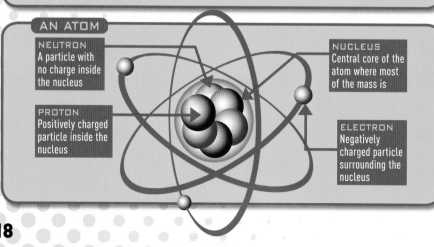

AN ATOM

NEUTRON
A particle with no charge inside the nucleus

PROTON
Positively charged particle inside the nucleus

NUCLEUS
Central core of the atom where most of the mass is

ELECTRON
Negatively charged particle surrounding the nucleus

SOME OF THE METEORITES FOUND IN CRATERS ON EARTH ARE EVEN OLDER THAN EARTH ROCKS. METEOR CRATER IN ARIZONA IS ONE OF THE FEW PLACES ON EARTH WHERE YOU CAN ACTUALLY SEE AN IMPACT CRATER.

WELL, THERE YOU HAVE IT, A SHORT TRIP BACK TO THE BEGINNING OF OUR PLANET. NOW I THINK IT'S TIME TO DO A LITTLE ROCK HUNTING OF MY OWN!

DIRTMEISTER'S NUGGET

THE OLDEST KNOWN ROCKS THAT HAVE BEEN DISCOVERED ON EARTH ARE SEVERAL ZIRCON CRYSTALS THAT COME FROM WESTERN AUSTRALIA. THESE REMARKABLE ROCK FRAGMENTS COME IN AT ABOUT 4,360,000,000 YEARS OLD.

MINERAL CRYSTALS ARE HABIT-FORMING

If you don't want to be one of those unlucky people who is fooled by fool's gold, then there are a few basic facts about minerals that you've got to know!

Most rocks are made out of **minerals.** You can think of them as being the building blocks of rocks. Some rocks are made of only one type of mineral and others are made up of many different minerals put together. So far, geologists have identified close to 3,000 different types of minerals, each with its own set of **properties.** Properties are features that can be used to describe or identify an object.

Let's see how gold and pyrite compare with each other when it comes to some of their properties.

COLOR: Gold and pyrite have a similar golden color, but it turns out that many different minerals can have the same color. To make it more confusing, some minerals, such as quartz, can come in lots of colors. Quartz can be black, purple, pink, and even clear. So color is not a great property to use to identify minerals.

SHAPE: Scientists call the shape of a mineral's crystal the **crystal habit,** and it's one of the most important properties for telling one mineral from another. Not all minerals form crystals but when they do, the crystals of the same mineral always look similar.

So, you are probably wondering why different minerals have different crystal habits. Like everything else in the universe, minerals are made of atoms. When a crystal grows, atoms join together in a process called bonding. Bonding is sort of like when you snap together building blocks to make some type of a structure. The blocks can't go together any old way. There are places for them to connect and rules that you need to follow to put them together. The same thing happens with atoms.

BECAUSE OF ITS COLOR, PYRITE IS OFTEN MISTAKEN FOR REAL GOLD.

MOST OFTEN REAL GOLD JUST FORMS RANDOM LUMPS. IT IS ALSO MUCH SOFTER AND HEAVIER THAN PYRITE.

THESE SPECTACULAR CRYSTALS ARE OF THE MINERAL AMETHYST, A TYPE OF PURPLE QUARTZ.

HALITE, OR COMMON TABLE SALT, IS ONE OF THE FEW MINERALS THAT WE EAT IN ITS CRYSTAL FORM. IF YOU LOOK AT SALT GRAINS WITH A MAGNIFYING GLASS YOU WILL SEE THAT THEY ALMOST ALWAYS HAVE SQUARE EDGES.

DON'T KNOCK THE HALITE OFF MY PRETZEL, DIGGER!

ATOMIC MODEL OF A SALT CRYSTAL
Most of the time salt crystals look like little cubes because they are made up of two different atoms, sodium (Na) and chlorine (Cl). The crystals have this special shape because of the way the atoms join together.

23

BREAKING UP IS HARD TO DO

If you have ever tried banging rocks together then you've probably noticed that some rocks are harder to break than others. This is no accident! It turns out that minerals have two properties that control the way they break. The first is called cleavage, and it describes how a mineral splits when it is hit. Not all minerals have cleavage, but those that do break along flat surfaces.

If you take a big chunk of halite and whack it with a hammer, it will usually break up into little cubes with square edges. Now if you hit a piece of mica with a hammer it will usually just bend, but you can use your finger to actually peel it into thin layers or sheets.

Not all minerals have a special way of breaking, though. If you take a piece of quartz and smack it with a hammer it will shatter like a piece of glass. When minerals break in a random way they don't have cleavage. Instead, geologists say that they fracture.

> Cleavage and fracture are properties that describe how a mineral will break apart.

Another property, hardness, describes how tough a mineral is. Basically hardness lets you know how easy it is to scratch a mineral. Some minerals, such as talc (you know, the stuff they make baby powder from), are so soft that you can scratch them with your fingernail. Others, like diamond, are so hard that they can be used to cut through steel. Diamonds will always be superhard, and talc will always be really soft. It turns out that hardness is one of the best properties to use to identify a mineral because it never changes. Geologists really like it when things stay constant!

Back in the early 1800s, a mineralogist named Friedrich Mohs was the first to classify minerals based on their hardness. These days, the Mohs' scale of mineral hardness is one of the most important tools that geologists use when it comes to identifying minerals.

BIO FRIEDRICH MOHS The Hardness of Minerals

BIRTHPLACE: GERMANY   BIRTH YEAR: 1773

Friedrich Mohs worked as a foreman of a mine, but his big break came when a banker hired him to work with his personal collection of minerals. The collection had many unknown minerals in it, and at that time there was no real good way to sort them out. Mohs examined the properties of the minerals and discovered that some were much harder than others. He ranked them based on which mineral could scratch the other. He then put the minerals into 10 groups with 1 being the soft minerals and 10 being the hardest. The Mohs' scale of hardness was born!

MOHS' SCALE OF HARDNESS »

RATING	MINERAL NAME	EXAMPLES
1	TALC	BAR OF SOAP
2	GYPSUM	FINGERNAIL
3	CALCITE	COPPER PENNY
4	FLUORITE	SOFT IRON NAIL
5	APATITE	STEEL POCKETKNIFE BLADE
6	ORTHOCLASE	WINDOW GLASS
7	QUARTZ	HARDENED STEEL FILE
8	TOPAZ	TOPAZ
9	CORUNDUM	RUBY, SAPPHIRE
10	DIAMOND	DIAMOND

BECAUSE IT **SPLITS** INTO THIN SHEET PIECES, **MICA** WAS USED AS WINDOWS IN POTTERY KILNS. THESE DAYS IT'S ALSO USED FOR MAKING **TINY INSULATORS** IN **ELECTRONIC** COMPONENTS SUCH AS **RESISTORS.**

Quartz can easily scratch softer minerals like calcite.

WATCH ME JUGGLE THESE RESISTORS WHILE MY MUG IS BAKING.

25

TAKING A SHINE TO MINERALS

Minerals come in a rainbow of colors. For that reason, it can be hard to figure out what a particular chunk of mineral is by looking at its **color** alone. Fortunately there are a few properties tied to a mineral's color that can be helpful in identifying it.

You've probably noticed that some rocks sparkle in the sunlight while others look dull and plain. This could be because a rock is covered in dirt, but often the difference has to do with a mineral property called **luster.** A mineral's luster describes the way that light bounces off of its surface.

Let's take a look at our old friend shiny pyrite again. Because it shines like metal, pyrite is said to have a **metallic luster.** If you look at a quartz crystal you'll see that the edges reflect light just like a piece of glass, so quartz is said to have a **vitreous luster.** "Vitreous" is a word that comes from the Latin word *vitrum*, which means "glass." When it comes to luster, most of the terms that are used are simply common descriptions of how the mineral looks. Some other luster terms are pearly, earthy, silky,

> The color of a mineral's streak is often different from the mineral's color.

greasy, sleepy, and bashful. OK, I made up the last two. Are you paying attention? You get the idea—when it comes to luster, it's all about the mineral's look.

GLOW, GLOW: Most of the time when we look at minerals we see them in sunlight or under some type of lamp that makes "white light." Things can get very interesting, though, when you switch to "black light." Black light is the common name for a special type of light called ultraviolet. Under ultraviolet light certain minerals glow and give off very different colors. Geologists call this property **fluorescence.** Take the mineral willemite, for example. When you look at it under normal white light, it looks pretty boring. When you hit it with ultraviolet light, though, it starts glowing with an eerie green color.

STREAKING AWAY: Over the years geologists have learned that many minerals have one color when they are in a crystal form but a different color when they get turned into a powder. Pyrite and gold both look like yellowish gold metals when they are solid. If you take the gold and rub it against a white porcelain tile, the mark it leaves behind will be gold. If you rub pyrite on the same tile, the mark will be black! Geologists call this property streak, and the special tile they use to test it is called a streak plate.

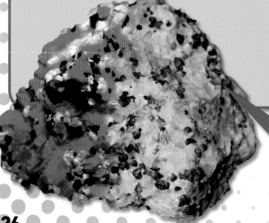

This rock contains the minerals willemite and franklinite. The left side of the photo shows the rock in ultraviolet light while the right side is under regular white light. The red and green colors come from these two fluorescent minerals.

Quartz crystals are said to have a vitreous luster because they look like glass.

Even though this hematite is black it leaves a reddish streak.

IT TURNS OUT THAT YOU CAN'T USE THE **STREAK TEST** ON ALL MINERALS BECAUSE SOME ARE TOO HARD. **ON MOHS' SCALE** OF HARDNESS A TYPICAL STREAK PLATE COMES IN **AROUND 7.** IF YOU TRY TO TAKE THE STREAK OF A SUPERHARD MINERAL SUCH AS **TOPAZ** OR **DIAMOND** YOU WIND UP SCRATCHING THE STREAK PLATE INSTEAD.

OOPS! LOOKS LIKE THAT WILL LEAVE A SCRATCH.

This sample of malachite looks green and also leaves a greenish streak.

HEAVY METALS AND ROCKS THAT GO FIZZ

If you've ever thrown stones into a pond you've probably noticed that some rocks feel heavier than others, and it's not just a size thing. Sometimes a small rock can actually weigh more than a large rock. That's because of their **density.** Density is a measure of how much an object weighs compared with the amount of space it takes up. If you take a lead fishing sinker and a piece of wood that are the same size, the sinker would be much heavier because lead has a higher density than wood. Most types of wood float when you put them in water, but lead will sink.

When geologists measure the density of a mineral they use the term **specific gravity.** Specific gravity is the density of a mineral compared with water. They don't do this just to complicate things. They compare minerals with water because water can be found any-where—all over the planet. Pure water has a density of 1 gram per cubic centimeter, so if a mineral has a specific gravity of 3 it sim-ply means that it is three times denser than water.

This sample of aragonite looks solid, but if you place it in acid it will dissolve.

Most minerals have specific gravities that range from 2.5 to about 4.5. If you measure a chunk of galena, though, you would find that it has a specific gravity of about 7.5. This is because galena contains lead, which is a very heavy metal. When it comes to specific gravity the champion is gold, which has a specific gravity of 19!

Getting Stuck on Minerals

One of the coolest properties can be found in the mineral magnetite. Magnetite has lots of iron in it, and as you might have guessed from the name, it is also magnetic. If you bring a steel paper clip near a piece of magnetite it will stick. The mineral magnetite is also called lodestone, which is an old English word that means "leading stone." The name comes from the fact that people would use lodestones to tell which direction they were heading in.

Tasty, Stinky, and Fizzy!

Most minerals have the same common prop-erties, but there are always a few oddballs! The mineral halite, for example, tastes salty because that's what it is (halite = salt). It's probably not a good idea for you to lick rocks, though, because some minerals are also poi-sonous! (Plus they are usually covered in dirt, which makes them taste yucky.) Sulfur is another mineral that is easy to identify because it has a bright yellow color and smells like rotten eggs. Then there are the carbonate minerals, including calcite, dolo-mite, and aragonite. These minerals are found in many common rocks, including limestone and marble, and they all fizz when you put acid on them. You can see this for yourself by doing a simple experiment.

When a drop of acid is placed on limestone it begins to bubble and fizz.

Magnetite is a naturally magnetic mineral, so objects made of steel will be attracted to it.

PEOPLE IN THE PAST DISCOVERED THAT IF YOU **HUNG A PIECE OF MAGNETITE** FROM A STRING IT WOULD ALWAYS WIND UP POINTING **NORTH,** SO THEY USED THESE HANGING ROCKS AS **SIMPLE COMPASSES.**

SO NOW YOU'RE TRYING TO BECOME A LIVING COMPASS, DIGGER?

TRY THIS! 🧪 THE ACID TEST

WHAT YOU'LL NEED

2 small pieces of chalk
2 large disposable plastic cups
A bottle of white vinegar

WHAT YOU'LL DO

Label one cup "water" and the second cup "acid." Place your carbonate mineral (a piece of chalk!) in the bottom of each cup and fill the cup labeled acid about halfway with vinegar. Fill the other cup about halfway with water. Watch what happens to the chalk in each cup when the liquid is first poured. Then place both cups in a safe location. After an hour or two has passed, look at the cups again. The chalk in the cup marked water should look pretty much the same as it did when you started. The chalk in the vinegar cup should have dissolved. This happens because vinegar is really a weak form of acid.

GEMS OF OUR ROCKY WORLD

The most awesome examples of mineral crystals are **gemstones.** A gem is a mineral that has extra value because of the way it looks. Most gems have three things going for them that make them stand out from ordinary minerals. First, they usually have flashy colors or dazzling **luster.** Second, most gems tend to be **harder** than other minerals. Finally, gemstones are usually rare. There are about 20 different minerals that can produce gemstones. Emerald and aquamarine are forms of the mineral beryl. Rubies and sapphires are pretty varieties of the common mineral corundum. Of course, diamonds are very rare, and what's rarer still is to find a diamond that has the properties needed to make a perfect gem. Most of the diamonds that are discovered never make it to the jewelry store. Instead, they are used to make special drill bits and saw blades that are used for cutting through rock. This is diamond's reward for being the hardest mineral!

Before gems are turned into jewelry or used for decorations, they need to be polished and cut. Polishing a stone will get rid of the rough spots on the surface of the stone and make it truly sparkle in the light.

Things get really tricky, though, when it comes to cutting and shaping gems, especially diamonds. Since diamond is the hardest mineral on Earth, it takes a lot of skill and some specialized techniques to cut. The first method that was used is called **cleaving**.

Even though diamonds are superhard, they can be split along certain directions. When cleaving a diamond, the jeweler uses a large flat blade with a sharp edge. The edge of the blade is placed into a small groove that is made on the surface of the diamond, usually with another diamond. He then takes a heavy mallet and whacks the back of the blade, and if all goes well, the diamond will split, leaving a perfectly smooth face. Of course, if things aren't lined up exactly right, the diamond could shatter like a piece of glass.

> A lapidary is a person who cuts and polishes gems.

BIO JOSEPH ASSCHER Rock Star

BIRTHPLACE: THE NETHERLANDS   BIRTH YEAR: 1871

Joseph Asscher was already a "rock star" of the diamond industry when, in 1908, he was presented with the biggest challenge of his life. Several years earlier, miners had discovered a whopping 3,106-carat diamond known as the Cullinan diamond. The diamond was as big as a man's fist but was very rough. It belonged to King Edward VII of England, and Asscher was given the job of finishing it. Asscher studied the diamond for three months, deciding on the best approach for cutting the stone. When he set the cleaving blade on the diamond, he held his breath and struck it with his mallet. To his astonishment, the diamond didn't split, but the blade did because the stone was too big for the blade. Asscher got a larger blade and struck the stone again. This time it split into three perfect pieces. These three sections were further cut, producing 9 large diamonds and about 100 smaller ones, which are part of the crown jewels of England.

DIAMONDS AND OTHER GEMSTONES ARE **MEASURED** IN UNITS CALLED **CARATS.** WHILE IT SOUNDS THE SAME, THESE HAVE NOTHING TO DO WITH THE **ORANGE-COLORED VEGETABLE** ... ONE CARAT IS EQUAL TO **0.2** GRAMS OR **200** MILLIGRAMS (.007 OZ).

CULLINAN DIAMOND

NO, DIGGER! NOT THAT KIND OF CARROT.

CHAPTER 3

EARTHQUAKES AND THEIR ORIGINS

WHAT EARTHQUAKES TELL US

1 HEY, DIGGER, I BET YOUR PALS WISH THEY HAD ONE OF THESE TO MAKE TUNNELS. THEY CERTAINLY DIG FASTER THAN PAWS!

2 CAREFUL WITH THAT SEISMIC SENSOR, DIGGER. WE DON'T WANT TO BREAK IT BEFORE WE GET IT HOOKED UP TO THE NETWORK.

4 WHAT'S THAT NOISE? KEEP IT DOWN OUT THERE, DIGGER. IT LOOKS LIKE SOMEONE IS TRYING TO REACH ME. THIS IS THE DIRTMEISTER, HOW CAN I HELP YOU?

5 HI, DIRTMEISTER, WHAT'S SHAKING? MY NAME IS KIM, AND I LIVE IN JAPAN. THE OTHER DAY WE HAD A SMALL EARTHQUAKE, AND IT GOT ME THINKING, WHAT CAUSES EARTHQUAKES AND DO THEY HAPPEN IN OTHER PLACES OR JUST HERE?

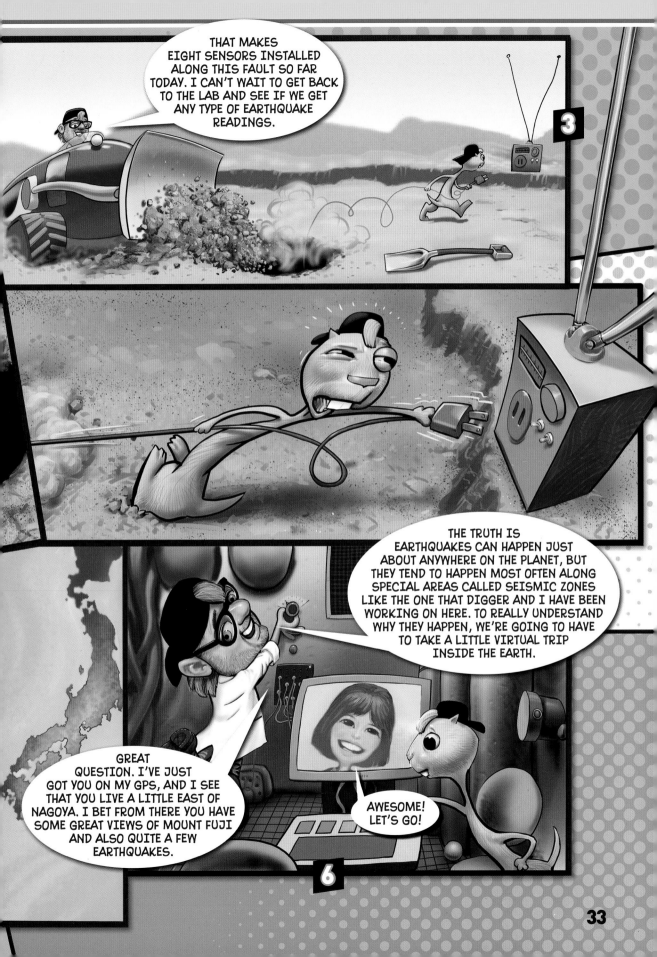

THERE'S A WHOLE LOT OF SHAKING GOING ON!

Did you know that there are over one million **earthquakes** each year? Most of the time they are so small you don't even notice them, though in some cases they feel like a truck or a train passing by. An earthquake happens when the ground begins to shake and energy is released beneath the surface. This makes the ground move up and down and back and forth.

A lot of different things can cause an earthquake. It might be the eruption of a nearby volcano, or the collapse of an underground cave. While most earthquakes are small and just affect a little area, when a major earthquake hits, it's usually because of stuff that's happening deep inside the planet.

It turns out that our Earth is not one solid chunk. It is made up of different layers of rock. The outermost layer is called the **crust,** and it has lots of cracks in it called **faults**. In many cases you can't see the faults at the surface because they are filled in with dirt, grass, or trees, or pavement covers them. Faults are the places where pieces of the crust can move past each other. And, when the crust moves, we have an earthquake!

The place on the fault where the rocks actually move is usually located many miles below the ground. The location on the surface directly above this point is called the **epicenter** of the earthquake. Forces acting inside the planet cause pressure to build up on the rocks on either side of the fault. Eventually the pressure gets so big that the rocks move, causing the ground around the fault to shake.

> Seismologists are geologists who specialize in the study of earthquakes.

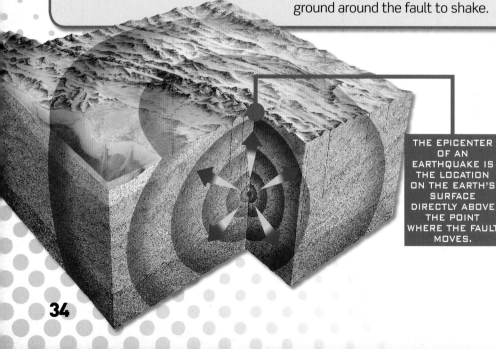

THE EPICENTER OF AN EARTHQUAKE IS THE LOCATION ON THE EARTH'S SURFACE DIRECTLY ABOVE THE POINT WHERE THE FAULT MOVES.

THE SAN ANDREAS IS A LARGE FAULT IN CALIFORNIA. OVER TIME, ROCKS ON OPPOSITE SIDES OF THE FAULT SLIDE PAST EACH OTHER.

DIRTMEISTER'S NUGGET

AN EARTHQUAKE IS USUALLY FOLLOWED BY A BUNCH OF SMALLER EARTHQUAKES CALLED **AFTERSHOCKS.** AFTERSHOCKS OCCUR BECAUSE THE PLACE WHERE THE **ROCKS MEET ON OPPOSITE SIDES** OF A FAULT IS NOT ALWAYS A SMOOTH SURFACE. SO THE ROCKS **GET STUCK. THE ENERGY** THAT IS RELEASED IN THE FIRST EARTHQUAKE GETS **PASSED ALONG THE FAULT,** CAUSING THE GROUND TO MOVE IN OTHER PLACES.

WOW, DIGGER, THIS EARTHQUAKE IS BETTER THAN A ROLLER COASTER!

CATCH A WAVE

In an earthquake, **waves** of energy move out through the surrounding rock and they eventually reach the surface. These waves are what cause the ground to shake back and forth. To better understand the way a wave works, let's look at a type that you are probably familiar with: water waves.

When you toss a rock into the water it makes a splash. Then you see circles moving out from where the rock hit. These are the waves. The first waves are the biggest. As the waves spread out they get smaller because they lose some of their energy as they move through the water. The best way to see how a wave behaves is to make some waves of your own! (See below.)

Earthquakes actually make different types of waves. Each of these waves travels in a unique way. To a seismologist the two most important are called **P waves and S waves.** The main difference between these two types of waves is the way that they shake the rocks that they move through.

P waves stands for "primary waves" because they travel the fastest from the site of an earthquake. P waves shake the Earth in the same direction that they move. Imagine a big spring like a Slinky stretched out on the floor. If you pull some of the coils together at one end and then let them go, you will see a wave pass through the spring as some of the coils get closer together and others get stretched farther apart.

S waves are "secondary waves." They travel more slowly than primary waves. As the S wave moves through the ground, the rocks move up and down. S waves are the same type of waves as those produced in the experiment below, and they are the same kind you would find moving through the water.

When you throw a rock into a pond it makes waves similar to the S waves created by earthquakes.

TRY THIS! 🌡 MAKING WAVES

WHAT YOU'LL NEED

A piece of rope about 10 feet (3 m) long
A chair, doorknob, or friend to hold the other end of the rope

WHAT YOU'LL DO

Tie one end of a rope to the back of a chair or doorknob or have a friend hold it. Stretch the rope out so that it does not touch the floor, but don't pull it so tight that you won't be able to move it up and down. Start by giving the rope a small snap up and down and observe the wave that travels through the rope. Now give the rope a bigger snap so that you are using more energy to pull it up and down. You should see a much larger wave move through the rope this time. The more energy that is used, the greater the height of the wave produced. Experiment to see how many different waves you can make. Try shaking the rope fast and slow to see how quickly the waves move. When you're done experimenting make sure you untie the rope from the door—you don't want to accidentally trip someone!

P WAVES

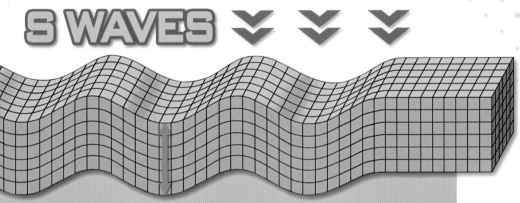

THE PRIMARY WAVES CAUSED BY AN EARTHQUAKE TRAVEL IN THE SAME DIRECTION AS THE ROCK PARTICLES VIBRATE, OR MOVE BACK AND FORTH.

S WAVES

THE SECONDARY WAVES CAUSED BY AN EARTHQUAKE TRAVEL IN ONE DIRECTION WHILE THE ROCK PARTICLES VIBRATE, OR MOVE BACK AND FORTH, IN A DIFFERENT DIRECTION.

DIRTMEISTER'S NUGGET

IN ADDITION TO **P WAVES** AND **S WAVES** EARTHQUAKES ALSO PRODUCE **SURFACE WAVES.** SURFACE WAVES FORM WHEN P WAVES AND S WAVES REACH THE SURFACE AND CAUSE THE GROUND TO SHAKE, AND THEY USUALLY CAUSE **MOST OF THE DAMAGE** TO BUILDINGS AND OTHER STRUCTURES.

WOW, DIGGER! I NEVER THOUGHT WE COULD SURF ON EARTHQUAKE WAVES!

MEASURING EARTHQUAKES

Some earthquakes are so strong that they knock down bridges and swallow cars, but others are so small we can barely feel them. Over the years scientists have come up with a few ways to measure the strength of an earthquake. The most common measurement used today is called the **Richter magnitude scale,** which tells how much energy was released when the earthquake struck. The scale starts at 1 and each whole number represents an increase in energy that is 32 times greater. This means that an earthquake with a magnitude of 4 is 32 times more powerful than an earthquake with a magnitude of 3. An earthquake of 5 is 32 times more powerful than a magnitude 4 but is over 1,000 times greater than a magnitude 3 (that's because 32 x 32 = 1,024).

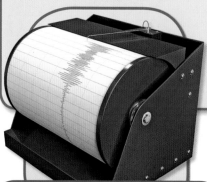

A seismograph is a device that measures the strength of the waves produced by an earthquake. The recording of the waves is called a seismogram.

This is a modern reproduction of one of the earliest devices built to detect earthquakes. It was made by the Chinese philosopher Zhang Heng back in A.D. 132.

BIO CHARLES RICHTER Man About Motion

BIRTHPLACE: UNITED STATES   BIRTH YEAR: 1900

Charles Richter was all about energy, and his main mission was to figure out what made earthquakes "tick." In 1927, he teamed up with a seismologist named Beno Gutenberg to study the physics of earthquakes.

After studying the problem for several years, Richter and Gutenberg decided they needed a standard way to measure the amount of energy released by an earthquake. After checking over the seismograms of many different earthquakes they realized that the more powerful an earthquake, the larger the line made by the S wave on the seismogram. This led to their developing the first earthquake magnitude scale. In 1935, Richter published their findings and to this day, whenever an earthquake hits, scientists remind us of the work of this Earth-shaking scientist by using his name!

WAVES FROM LARGE EARTHQUAKES CAN DESTROY ROADS.

DIRTMEISTER'S NUGGET

BECAUSE OF THE WAY THE RICHTER SCALE WORKS, ONLY THE LARGEST EARTHQUAKES EVER GET ABOVE MAGNITUDE 7. MOST PEOPLE CAN'T EVEN FEEL EARTHQUAKES THAT ARE MAGNITUDE 2 OR SMALLER. TO DATE, THE LARGEST EARTHQUAKE EVER RECORDED HAPPENED ON MAY 22, 1960, IN SOUTHERN CHILE. IT HAD A RICHTER MAGNITUDE OF 9.5!

HANG ON, DIGGER, HERE COMES A BIG ONE!

39

GETTING THE INSIDE STORY

Earthquakes can destroy things, but they also can provide scientists with some very useful information about what is going on inside the Earth. Earthquake waves bounce and bend when they travel from one type of rock into another. Also, some waves can travel through solids, but they cannot pass through liquids like water or **magma.** By studying the behavior of earthquake waves, seismologists can get an idea of how the different layers of rock stack up below the Earth's surface.

In the early 1900s, most geologists figured that the Earth was one solid chunk right through to the center of the planet. This view began to change when scientists noticed that the waves from large, distant earthquakes would sometimes

> Seismologists can use earthquake waves to "look" inside the Earth.

speed up or slow down. In other cases, waves would change direction or simply disappear. The only explanation for this was that the rocks on the inside of the planet were very different from the ones that we have near the surface.

It took almost 20 years, but scientists put together the picture of the inner planet that we pretty much use today. Instead of the Earth being one solid chunk of rock, it is actually made up of four main layers. At the center is a dense, solid **inner core** made up of some heavy metals, including iron and nickel. Surrounding that is the **outer core,** which is also made of metals, but they are mostly in the form of a liquid. Surrounding the two cores is the thickest layer, called the **mantle.** The mantle is made of very dense rock and it is technically a solid, but it has soft areas so it can flow over time. Finally, the outermost layer is the **crust,** which is made of solid rock that is fairly brittle.

According to the current theory, it is the movement of rocks in the upper mantle and lower crust that causes most big earthquakes. As these rocks slowly move, the rocks along the fault begin to slide past each other and there is an earthquake.

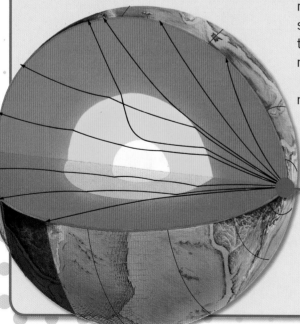

EARTHQUAKE WAVES IN THE EARTH:
Earthquake waves often change speed and direction as they move from one layer of the Earth to the next.

INTERNAL STRUCTURE OF THE EARTH

THE EARTH IS NOT ONE SOLID MASS, BUT IS MADE UP OF FOUR MAIN LAYERS.

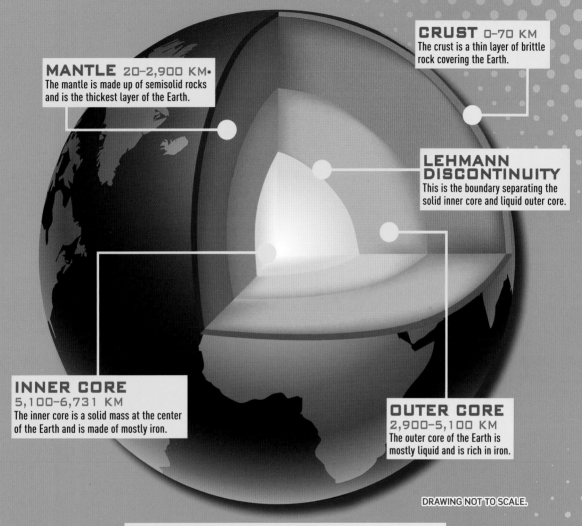

CRUST 0–70 KM
The crust is a thin layer of brittle rock covering the Earth.

MANTLE 20–2,900 KM*
The mantle is made up of semisolid rocks and is the thickest layer of the Earth.

LEHMANN DISCONTINUITY
This is the boundary separating the solid inner core and liquid outer core.

INNER CORE
5,100–6,731 KM
The inner core is a solid mass at the center of the Earth and is made of mostly iron.

OUTER CORE
2,900–5,100 KM
The outer core of the Earth is mostly liquid and is rich in iron.

DRAWING NOT TO SCALE.

*Note that the crust under the ocean is thinner than the crust under the continents—the depth to the mantle varies depending on the location.

BIO INGE LEHMANN UNRAVELS THE CORE

BIRTHPLACE: DENMARK BIRTH YEAR: 1888

One of the first people to "see" inside the Earth was Inge Lehmann. Even though there were very few women geologists at that time, Inge became an expert in reading seismograms, and in 1928 she was given the job of chief of seismology for the Royal Danish Geodetic Institute.

Over the next eight years, Lehmann conducted detailed studies of seismograms, and she discovered that the P waves coming from very deep earthquakes seemed to be bouncing off of a layer inside the Earth's core. She concluded that the only explanation for this unusual behavior was that the core had two parts to it: a small solid inner core in the center surrounded by a larger liquid core. She published her findings in 1936, and in honor of her amazing discovery the layer between the inner and outer core is now called the Lehmann discontinuity.

PREDICTING "THE BIG ONE"

One of the reasons that scientists are so interested in studying earthquakes is because they can be extremely dangerous to people. When the ground starts shaking, anything attached to it also starts to move. Buildings, bridges, and roads may fall apart. Gas and water lines can also break. Another problem with earthquakes is that in hilly areas they can trigger landslides, which can bury houses and roads, block streams, and cause flooding.

Floods can also happen because of **tsunamis.** A tsunami is a giant wave that occurs as a result of an earthquake under the sea or along the coast. Tsunamis can travel across the ocean and wipe out entire towns that are located far from the place where the earthquake happened.

Being Safe in an Earthquake

One of the biggest problems with earthquakes is that they usually happen without any warning. This makes them very different from hurricanes, blizzards, or even tornadoes, for which scientists can give people a heads-up to prepare. If geologists could come up with a way to give people even a few minutes of notice before an earthquake hits, it could save many lives. Unfortunately, as of yet there are no good ways of predicting exactly when or where an earthquake will happen.

Scientists are working on the problem, though. By making maps of active faults, geologists can get an idea of where an earthquake might hit. The way they do this is to plot where earthquakes have happened in the past and then connect the dots!

The other thing about earthquakes is that they tend to happen in bunches, so if one strikes along a fault, then there is a good possibility that there will be some aftershocks in the same area. Of course, the best way to be safe in an earthquake is to know what to do and where to go when one hits. That's why in places like Japan, which has lots of earthquakes, kids in schools go through earthquake drills.

> Some of the biggest dangers in earthquakes are from falling buildings.

EARTHQUAKE ACTIVITY AROUND THE WORLD

THE DOTS ON THIS MAP SHOW THE LOCATION OF THE EPICENTERS OF ALL MAGNITUDE 5 AND GREATER EARTHQUAKES THAT HAPPENED AROUND THE WORLD OVER ONE YEAR.

In some cases, earthquake waves can destroy buildings.

Earthquakes that happen under the ocean can cause tsunamis.

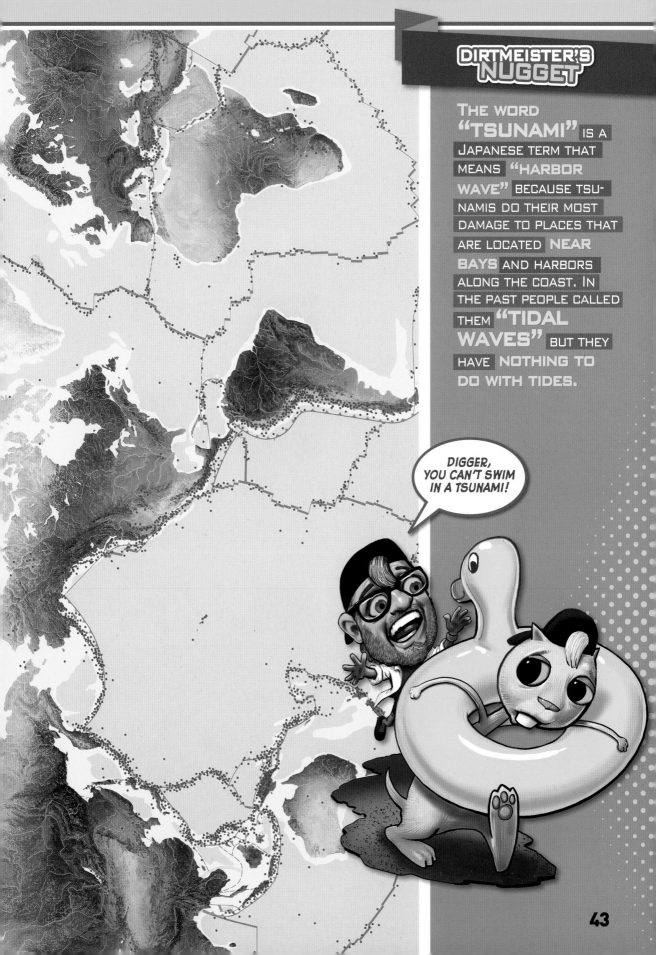

THE WORD **"TSUNAMI"** IS A JAPANESE TERM THAT MEANS "HARBOR WAVE" BECAUSE TSUNAMIS DO THEIR MOST DAMAGE TO PLACES THAT ARE LOCATED **NEAR BAYS** AND HARBORS ALONG THE COAST. IN THE PAST PEOPLE CALLED THEM **"TIDAL WAVES"** BUT THEY HAVE **NOTHING TO DO WITH TIDES.**

DIGGER, YOU CAN'T SWIM IN A TSUNAMI!

LOOK OUT! HOT STUFF BELOW!

You don't want to be stuck next to a volcano when the Earth begins to spew forth gobs of super-hot stuff. So what exactly is a volcano? A volcano is an opening in the Earth's crust through which eruptions take place.

There are many types of volcanoes. Most produce lava, which is hot melted rock that starts as magma and shoots out from deep underground. Most volcanoes also release gases, some of which are poisonous. They can also produce steam and water. Many volcanoes blast out volcanic ash, which is a fine hot dust. Some even blow out big chunks of rocks called volcanic bombs.

So how does magma form in the first place? Well, it turns out that in the crust and upper mantle there are pockets of rock that have a bunch of radioactive elements. These produce lots of heat and turn the surrounding rock into magma. The area directly under the volcano where the magma collects is called the magma chamber.

After the magma chamber forms, the melted rock works its way to the surface. The reason magma rises is because it is less dense than the surrounding rock. Density is a measure of how much weight an object has compared with the amount of space it takes up. You can see how liquid magma rises due to a change in density by trying a simple experiment.

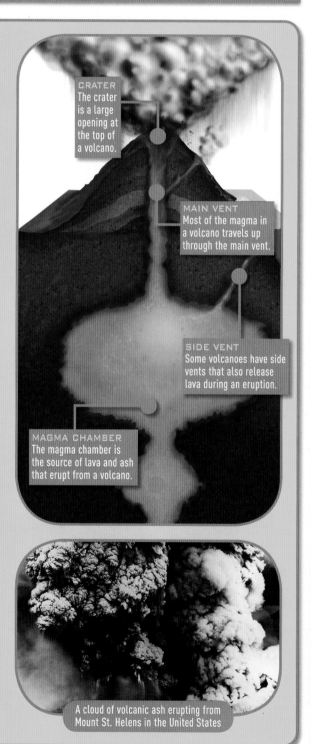

CRATER
The crater is a large opening at the top of a volcano.

MAIN VENT
Most of the magma in a volcano travels up through the main vent.

SIDE VENT
Some volcanoes have side vents that also release lava during an eruption.

MAGMA CHAMBER
The magma chamber is the source of lava and ash that erupt from a volcano.

A cloud of volcanic ash erupting from Mount St. Helens in the United States

A VOLCANIC ERUPTION WITH A RIVER OF HOT LAVA

TRY THIS!
MAGMA ON THE MOVE

WHAT YOU'LL NEED

A clear plastic bottle
Some red food coloring
A clear plastic straw
A lump of modeling clay
A portable hair dryer

WHAT YOU'LL DO

Grab an adult to help you with this experiment. Put a few drops of food coloring in the bottom of the bottle and then fill it about three-quarters full with cool water. Place the straw in the bottle so that the bottom of the straw is about two inches (5 cm) under the water and the top is sticking out of the bottle. Pack the clay around the straw at the top of the bottle so that you seal the top of the bottle around the straw. You want to make this seal as tight as possible so that no water leaks out of the bottle around the straw and no air gets in. Observe the level of the water in the straw. Turn on the hair dryer and set it so that it is on low but it still has warm air blowing out of it. Hold the hair dryer a few inches away from the bottle and point it so the warm air is blowing on the middle of the bottle. Watch how the water rises through the straw as the water in the bottle gets warmer. Be careful not to heat the water too much or else you might get an unplanned eruption from the top of the straw!

The water in the bottle acts just like magma when it gets hot.

VOLCANOES AROUND THE WORLD

After watching volcanoes blow their top for a few hundred years, geologists have discovered that there are three basic types of volcanoes. They've learned that the differences between them are caused by the type of magma that they are made from.

Felsic magmas tend to be light colored and they are really gooey and sticky. Volcanoes containing felsic magma usually have a great deal of gas trapped in them so they tend to be explosive when they erupt.

Mafic magmas are usually dark colored and are much thinner than felsic magmas. The lava they produce flows very easily so they are not usually explosive. When these volcanoes erupt the lava simply flows down the side of the volcano like a hot river of molten rock.

Many volcanoes don't even erupt lava. Instead they release layer upon layer of ash, which produces a volcano with really steep sides. This type of volcano is called a cinder cone.

A composite cone is made from both lava and ash. These different types of layers can build a very tall mountain, often reaching over 8,000 feet (2,400 m)!

> Cinder cones, composite cones, and shield cones are different types of volcanoes.

Composite cones are usually found along the edge of continents and include some of the most famous volcanoes in the world, such as Mount Fuji in Japan and Mount St. Helens in the United States.

Composite cone volcanoes are also the most dangerous because they tend to be very explosive. In some cases, the magma cools off and turns solid inside the volcano, forming a plug. This is like putting your finger on top of a bottle of soda and shaking it up. Sometimes the entire top of the mountain can blow off.

The third type of volcano is called a shield volcano and these are the most common in the world, although we don't always see them. That's because many shield volcanoes are found on the ocean floor. Shield volcanoes are broad and flat, but they can get really tall. Many of the islands that are found in the Pacific Ocean, including those that make up Hawaii, are the tops of shield volcanoes that have popped up through the surface of the sea. Shield volcanoes are rarely explosive because they are made from easy-flowing mafic magma. In many cases they will have spectacular lava fountains that are particularly cool to watch at night.

The Paricutin volcano is one of the largest cinder cone volcanoes in the world.

MOUNT HOOD IN OREGON IS A COMPOSITE CONE VOLCANO.

SNOW-COVERED TUNGURAHUA VOLCANO IN ECUADOR ERUPTS AT NIGHT, SHOWING LAVA FOUNTAINS.

LAVA FROM KILAUEA VOLCANO IN HAWAII STREAMS INTO THE OCEAN.

EVEN THOUGH **MOUNT EVEREST** IS THE HIGHEST MOUNTAIN IN THE WORLD, **IT IS NOT THE TALLEST.** IF YOU MEASURE THE **MAUNA KEA** VOLCANO IN HAWAII FROM ITS BASE TO THE SUMMIT, IT IS MORE THAN **4,000 FEET (1,200 M) TALLER** THAN MOUNT EVEREST. THE REASON MAUNA KEA DOESN'T GET THE TITLE OF HIGHEST MOUNTAIN ON EARTH IS THAT ONLY ABOUT **14,000 FEET (4,300 M) OF IT STICKS UP OUT OF THE OCEAN.** THE REST OF THE MOUNTAIN IS **UNDER WATER!**

YOU SWIM, I WILL NAP. I LOVE HAWAII.

HOT ROCKS

Whether it comes spewing out of a volcano as lava, or simply chills out deep under the Earth's surface, magma does not stay a hot liquid forever. Eventually it cools off and forms a solid rock. Geologists call the rocks that form from magma igneous rocks.

Igneous rocks are divided into two main groups. Extrusive igneous rocks form above the surface of the Earth and are found mostly near active and extinct volcanoes. Intrusive igneous rocks form below the Earth's surface.

Intrusive and extrusive igneous rocks look very different from each other even if they start off from the exact same type of magma. Some igneous rocks have a surface that is smooth like glass or bumpy and full of holes. Others have large crystals that have grown together.

Igneous rocks usually get large crystals in them if the magma that they form from cools really slowly. Igneous rocks with large crystals are almost always intrusive igneous rocks because magmas cool slowly when they are trapped underground.

When lava erupts from a volcano, it cools off pretty fast. This means that there is little time for minerals to form crystals. In many cases the only way to see the individual crystals in extrusive igneous rocks is by using a microscope.

Sometimes lava will cool so quickly that the rocks do not have any crystals at all. When this happens, geologists say that the rock has a glassy texture. One of the most common glassy igneous rocks is obsidian, which was often used by Native Americans to make arrowheads and cutting tools.

THIS DAGGER IS MADE FROM OBSIDIAN, A VOLCANIC GLASS WITH SHARP EDGES.

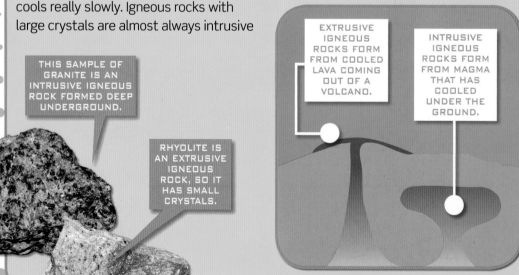

THIS SAMPLE OF GRANITE IS AN INTRUSIVE IGNEOUS ROCK FORMED DEEP UNDERGROUND.

RHYOLITE IS AN EXTRUSIVE IGNEOUS ROCK, SO IT HAS SMALL CRYSTALS.

EXTRUSIVE IGNEOUS ROCKS FORM FROM COOLED LAVA COMING OUT OF A VOLCANO.

INTRUSIVE IGNEOUS ROCKS FORM FROM MAGMA THAT HAS COOLED UNDER THE GROUND.

IF **LAVA** HAS A LOT OF **GAS BUBBLES** IN IT WHEN IT COOLS, THE BUBBLES WILL **GET TRAPPED** IN THE SOLID ROCK. THIS LEAVES THE ROCK WITH **A LOT OF HOLES** IN IT. ONE OF THE **COOLEST TYPES** OF ROCKS IS **PUMICE,** WHICH HAS SO MANY GAS BUBBLES IN IT THAT IT CAN ACTUALLY **FLOAT** IN WATER!

PUMICE IS A VOLCANIC ROCK THAT CAN FLOAT IN WATER.

NOW THAT'S A COOL WAY TO USE PUMICE, DIGGER!

SOMETHING IS COOKING IN THE CRUST

Since magma is churning and burning deep underground, a lot of the Earth's crust is made up of igneous rocks. This is not surprising because if the Earth formed from a hot ball of gas and dust, as most geologists believe, then as it cooled down, igneous rocks would have been the first type of rock to form.

Earlier we said that there are basically two main types of magmas cooking inside the Earth. Felsic magmas are light colored, while mafic magma is dark. As it turns out, there is another big difference between these two types of magmas. Rocks formed from mafic magma have a higher density than felsic rocks, so they are usually heavier.

If you look at where these two types of igneous rocks are found in the crust, it's easy to see a pattern. Most of the crust that makes up the ocean floor is made up of mafic rocks, while the continents are made of mostly felsic igneous rocks.

This is not simply a coincidence. Because mafic rocks are denser, they push deeper into the mantle. It works the same with wooden blocks and water. If you put a block made from maple and a block made from balsa wood into a big pan of water, the balsa wood would float higher because it is less dense.

Since felsic and mafic magmas contain different chemical elements, it stands to reason that they also will produce rocks with different minerals. Geologists use the minerals found in igneous rocks to put them into different family groups.

Almost three-quarters of the igneous rocks found in the Earth's crust are in the basalt family.

Basalt is a dark-colored mafic rock that is often found in lava flows on top of the Earth's surface. Much of the crust under the ocean is made of basalt and so are places like Hawaii and Iceland.

Then we have the granite family, which is at the opposite end of the spectrum from basalt. Rocks in the granite family are light-colored felsic rocks that are found only on continents.

> Most of the Earth's crust is formed from two types of igneous rocks.

MOST OF THE CONTINENTAL CRUST IS MADE OF LIGHT-COLORED FELSIC IGNEOUS ROCKS IN THE GRANITE FAMILY.

MOST OF THE OCEAN CRUST IS MADE OF DARK-COLORED MAFIC IGNEOUS ROCKS IN THE BASALT FAMILY.

FORMATION OF OCEANIC CRUST AND CONTINENTAL CRUST

CONTINENTAL CRUST
Most of the continents are made from low-density felsic rocks.

OCEANIC CRUST
Most of the crust under the oceans is made up of high-density mafic rocks.

MANTLE
The mantle is found beneath both types of crust.

NICE JOB, DIGGER. NOW I KNOW HOW YOU GOT YOUR NAME!

DIRTMEISTER'S NUGGET

THERE IS ONE LAST TYPE OF IGNEOUS ROCK, BUT IT IS ACTUALLY PRETTY RARE IN THE CRUST. KNOWN AS **ULTRAMAFIC ROCKS,** THESE SUPER-DENSE, DARK-COLORED ROCKS ARE CALLED **PERIDOTITE.** SOME GEOLOGISTS BELIEVE THAT THEY HAVE BEEN CARRIED TO THE CRUST BY **MAGMA** FLOWING UP FROM THE MANTLE!

HOT SPOTS AND THE RING OF FIRE

Ok, so where do you need to go if you want to find some volcanoes blowing their top? Like earthquakes, volcanoes don't happen randomly all over the planet. By far, the largest number of active volcanoes can be found along the edges of the continents surrounding the Pacific Ocean. Geologists call this zone the Ring of Fire.

Sometimes, as in Hawaii, a volcano will form in the middle of the ocean. These places are called hot spots, and the reason they exist is not really clear. Many geologists believe that hot spots happen because pockets of radioactive elements located in the upper mantle are cooking the rocks above, causing them to melt.

Volcanoes can also happen because of something called a rift eruption. Rifts are long cracks in the Earth's crust that allow magma to bubble up from below. These rift zones can be found on both the continents and on the ocean floor. Two of the most famous rift zones are the East African Rift Valley in Kenya and the Mid-Atlantic Ridge.

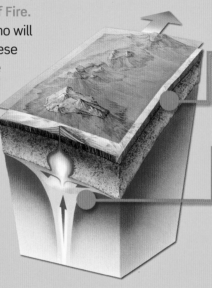

THE ISLANDS OF HAWAII ARE VOLCANOES THAT FORMED IN THE MIDDLE OF THE OCEAN.

THE MAGMA TO MAKE THESE VOLCANOES CAME FROM HOT SPOTS IN THE MANTLE BELOW THE CRUST.

BIO MAURICE & KATIA KRAFFT TRUE LOVE ON A VOLCANO

Volcanologists love adventure! After all, they climb active volcanoes while hot lava pours out of the top. That's exactly how Katia and Maurice Krafft made their living. Technically, the Kraffts were not scientists—they were filmmakers—but they did a lot to educate the world about the power and potential danger of volcanic eruptions.

Maurice and Katia's mission started when they took a trip to film the eruption of Stromboli, a volcano in Italy. The Kraffts went on to film hundreds of volcanic eruptions, often getting only a few feet from active lava flows that were well over 1832°F (1000°C).

They showed just how dangerous volcanic eruptions could be, and their work saved hundreds if not thousands of lives.

The Kraffts' careers came to an end in Spring 1991 when they traveled to Japan to film the eruption of Mount Unzen near the town of Shimabara. They thought they were in a safe area, but as is often the case with volcanoes, conditions quickly changed. The Kraffts were killed along with the rest of their team. Throughout their careers both Maurice and Katia knew the dangers that they faced, but their love of volcanoes and for each other kept them going.

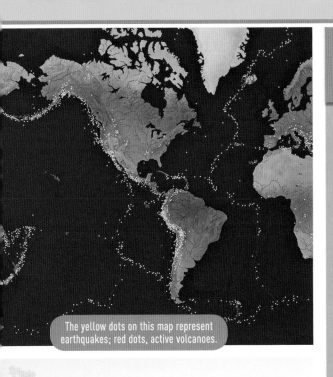

The yellow dots on this map represent earthquakes; red dots, active volcanoes.

DEADLY BLASTS FROM THE PAST

People have been dealing with the dangers of big volcanic blasts for tens of thousands of years. Here's a rundown of some of the deadliest volcanic eruptions that have been recorded so far.

About 1600 B.C. the volcanic island of Thera near Greece blew up, pretty much wiping out the Minoan civilization.

In 1669 Mount Etna in Italy erupted, killing about 40,000 people and leaving a crack in the surface of the Earth over six miles (9.5 km) long.

In 1815 Tambora volcano in Indonesia erupted, killing over 10,000 people. The eruption put so much dust in the air that the temperature of the Earth dropped 0.54°F (0.3°C), and 1816 became known as the Year Without a Summer.

In 1883 Krakatoa in Indonesia erupted, killing an estimated 36,000 people.

In 1902 at Mount Pelée on Martinique a fast-moving cloud of superheated gas raced down the side of the volcano, killing an estimated 30,000 people.

A view of Mount Etna smoking at sunrise

AFTER ALL THIS HOT INFORMATION ABOUT VOLCANOES, DIGGER AND I ARE GOING TO COOL OFF WITH A LITTLE DIP IN THE OCEAN. IT'S TIME TO HEAD FOR THE BEACH!

View of Mount Pelée on the island of Martinique

CHAPTER 5

SHIFTING PLATES AND DRIFTING CONTINENTS

THE SHAPE OF THE CONTINENTS

1 HEY, DIGGER, CHECK OUT THAT SEAMOUNT! I'M SURE GLAD THAT WE GOT THIS GIG MAPPING THE SEAFLOOR FOR THE FOLKS AT NOAA.

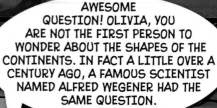

AWESOME QUESTION! OLIVIA, YOU ARE NOT THE FIRST PERSON TO WONDER ABOUT THE SHAPES OF THE CONTINENTS. IN FACT A LITTLE OVER A CENTURY AGO, A FAMOUS SCIENTIST NAMED ALFRED WEGENER HAD THE SAME QUESTION.

4 YO, DIRT DUDE...I'M SO GLAD I REACHED YOU! MY NAME IS OLIVIA AND I'M WITH MY PARENTS TAKING A CRUISE. WE JUST PASSED THROUGH THE PANAMA CANAL, AND I'VE BEEN FOLLOWING OUR ROUTE ON A BIG MAP OF THE WORLD. I NOTICED THAT THE CONTINENTS HAVE SOME INTERESTING SHAPES. DID THEY GET THAT WAY BY CHANCE OR IS THERE A REASON THAT THEY LOOK THE WAY THEY DO?

5

CONTINENTS ON THE MOVE

Are you any good at puzzles? If you are, take a look at a map of the world or a globe and you'll see that the continents make an interesting pattern. The coasts of Africa and South America seem to be mirror images of each other. The same can be said of the coasts of Europe and North America. Without too much trouble, it is easy to imagine them fitting back together like puzzle pieces to make one large continent.

Not long after Columbus made his historic voyages, people began drawing maps showing the Atlantic Ocean. This got them wondering about the shape of the continents. By the mid-1800s a number of scientists were coming up with theories trying to explain the "fit" of the continental coastlines. Some, such as Eduard Suess and James Dana, believed that the reason the coasts looked similar was that the Earth was slowly shrinking as it cooled off.

Antonio Snider-Pellegrini suggested that the continents had been ripped apart by some type of catastrophic event. In 1858 he published a map showing the continents assembled into one giant landmass, but few scientists took him seriously. Most geologists believed that the shape of the continents was simply a coincidence and they stopped looking for reasons. That's when Alfred Wegener came on the scene.

> Alfred Wegener introduced the idea of continental drift.

BIO ALFRED WEGENER — Drifting Continents

BIRTHPLACE: GERMANY   BIRTH YEAR: 1880

Not many people are strong enough to move continents, but that's exactly what Alfred Wegener tried to do! Wegener's main research was on climate, but he became interested in why the continents and oceans had the shapes that they did.

Wegener studied maps of the Earth and the different types of rocks found on each of the continents. He became convinced that at some point in the past all the continents were joined together into one giant supercontinent, which he called Pangaea. In 1915, he published a book called *The Origin of Continents and Oceans*, in which he explained his theory of continental drift.

At first, most of the geologists who had read it didn't believe him and refused to accept his work. Over time, though, his ideas led to the development of one of the most important theories in science today!

Unlike others who came before him, Alfred Wegener didn't just base his theory of continental drift on the fact that the continents had similar coastlines. Instead, he collected additional evidence from several different branches of science. At that time it was unusual to use different types of science to solve a problem. Today, this "interdisciplinary approach" is very common. In the end, Alfred Wegener not only came up with a theory to explain how the continents got their shapes, but he paved the way for modern scientists to think about a problem from many different angles.

CONTINENTAL DRIFT

IN 1915 ALFRED WEGENER CREATED A MAP OF THE WORLD, SIMILAR
TO THIS ONE, SHOWING HOW THE MODERN-DAY CONTINENTS COULD ALL FIT BACK
TOGETHER INTO A SINGLE GIANT CONTINENT CALLED PANGAEA.

EURASIA

NORTH AMERICA

AFRICA

SOUTH
AMERICA

INDIA

AUSTRALIA

ANTARCTICA

THE FLOW BELOW THE MOHO

The main problem with Alfred Wegener's theory of continental drift was that no one could explain how the continents could move around on the surface of the planet if the Earth was a solid chunk of rock. In the early 1900s, advances in seismology gave geologists a tool to look inside the Earth and this picture of a solid Earth began to change. Even before Inge Lehmann discovered the boundary between the inner and outer core, a Croatian scientist named Andrija Mohorovicic discovered the boundary between the Earth's mantle and crust.

Mohorovicic was a whiz in math and in 1892 he was put in charge of the national meteorological observatory, where he had the use of several seismographs. When a large earthquake hit the area in 1909, Mohorovicic discovered that several miles below the surface there was a sudden change in the speed of earthquake waves. This layer acted like a boundary that separated the hard brittle rocks of the crust from the softer rocks of the mantle below. Today, this boundary layer is officially called the Mohorovicic discontinuity, but most geologists simply refer to it as the Moho.

WELCOME TO THE ASTHENOSPHERE

After the discovery of the Moho, other scientists started using earthquake waves to take a look at what was happening deep inside the planet. They discovered that when the waves reached between 65 and 210 miles (105–338 km) below the surface, they began to slow down. The best explanation for the change in speed was that the rocks in this zone were not totally solid. The possibility that they were more like a superthick gooey fluid would explain the change in speed of the waves. After further research, geologists found that this was indeed the case, and they named this layer of the mantle the asthenosphere. Having a softer layer in the mantle that could flow solved the mystery of how continents could move! Today, the layer of solid rocks that make up the upper mantle and crust above is called the lithosphere.

Little by little the pieces in the continental drift puzzle were falling into place. Now all geologists had to do was figure out how the rocks of the lithosphere moved. The answer has to do with something called convection.

If you remember back to your rising-magma experiment you know that when a fluid gets hot, it expands and rises. As the fluid rises, it cools off again and sinks back down, forming a big loop called a convection current. Today, most geologists believe that it is these convection currents, powered by decaying radioactive elements, that drive the moving continents.

> The Moho is the name of the layer that separates the crust from the mantle below.

CONVECTION CURRENTS INSIDE THE EARTH

GEOLOGISTS BELIEVE THAT LARGE CONVECTION CURRENTS (SEEN HERE AS ARROWS) IN THE EARTH'S MANTLE CAUSE THE LITHOSPHERE ABOVE TO MOVE.

LITHOSPHERE

OUTER CORE

INNER CORE

LITHOSPHERE

ASTHENOSPHERE

MANTLE

THE ASTHENOSPHERE IS A LAYER OF **SOFT ROCK** FOUND IN THE UPPER MANTLE THAT CAN FLOW LIKE **SUPERTHICK TOOTHPASTE.** PIECES OF THE **LITHOSPHERE** ABOVE RIDE ON TOP OF THE ASTHENOSPHERE LIKE RAFTS **FLOATING ON WATER.**

WHAT ARE YOU DOING WITH THAT TOOTHPASTE, DIGGER?

MAKING THE MOUNTAINS

Have you ever wondered where mountains come from? With a volcano the answer is pretty simple. Magma bubbles up from inside the Earth, and each time the volcano erupts the mountain gets a little bigger. Depending on how often a volcano erupts a person could actually watch it grow over a few years.

Most mountains are not made from volcanoes. To make it even more of a puzzle, the rocks that make up many of the tallest mountains look as if they have been bent and twisted, and many have fossils of sea creatures in them. People usually explained the presence of these fossil shells by saying that they were carried there during Noah's flood. Back in the late 1400s, Leonardo da Vinci explained that the rocks that made mountains formed under the sea and then were pushed up.

With the discovery of the asthenosphere (the gooey, semisolid layer of the mantle), and the idea that the rocks of the crust could move around, the picture suddenly

> Leonardo da Vinci was one of the first people to explain how mountains formed.

became a little clearer. If the same forces that moved the continents away from each other at one place on the Earth pushed continents together somewhere else, the rocks that were stuck in between would have nowhere to go but up. Check out how this works in the experiment below.

Big Happenings Under the Sea

The oceans of the world have always been a big mystery! Until the 1950s, most people assumed that the ocean floor was as flat as a pancake. That view changed after World War I, when a tracking device called sonar was developed. Using sonar, an operator can figure out how far away an object is or what the ocean floor looks like. A geologist named Harry Hammond Hess first came up with the idea of using sonar to "see" what was going on at the bottom of the ocean. Scientists didn't really get the whole picture, though, until a pair of geologists named Marie Tharp and Bruce Heezen created the first accurate maps of the ocean floor.

TRY THIS! 🧪 Making Mountains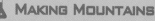

WHAT YOU'LL NEED

5 pieces of construction paper, each a different color if possible
A tabletop or similar smooth flat surface

WHAT YOU'LL DO

Stack the pieces of construction paper on the surface of the table. Place one hand on either side of the stack of paper and slowly move your hands closer together. As you do, you will see that the center of the stack begins to bend upward, forming a mini-mountain right before your eyes. Geologists call this force compression, and it is what caused most of the largest mountain chains to form. The different-colored papers will help you see what is happening below the surface.

This map produced by Marie Tharp in 1977 was the first accurate map of the Earth's entire seafloor.

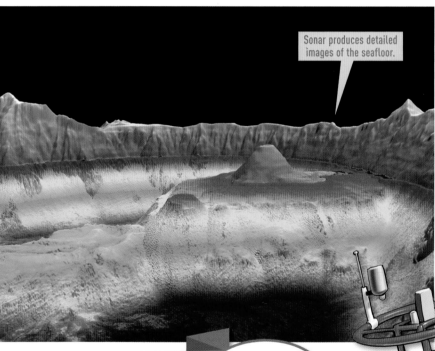

Sonar produces detailed images of the seafloor.

BIO
MARIE THARP

BIRTHPLACE: MICHIGAN, U.S.A.
BIRTH YEAR: 1920

Marie Tharp was never afraid to try new things and meet new people. In 1948 she moved to New York and went to work with Bruce Heezen, a marine geologist who was doing early studies of the ocean floor. The two would form a partnership that lasted almost 30 years. Heezen would go to sea and use sonar to collect data. Tharp used the data to make detailed drawings of the seafloor.

In 1952 she made the first ever 3-D map of the bottom of the Atlantic Ocean. Her map showed that there was a tall mountain chain running down the middle of the ocean and deep valleys running along the edges of many of the continents. These features, called the **mid-ocean ridge** and a **submarine trench,** provided key clues to how the continents could move.

DIRTMEISTER'S NUGGET

DO YOU SEE ANY MOUNTAINS AROUND HERE, DIGGER?

EVEN THOUGH WE CAN ONLY **SEE TINY BITS** OF IT WHERE IT STICKS UP OUT OF THE WATER, THE MID-OCEAN RIDGE IS THE **LONGEST MOUNTAIN** CHAIN ON EARTH. IT WINDS ITS WAY FOR OVER **45,000 MILES** (72,000 KM) ALONG THE SEAFLOOR AND IT TOUCHES EVERY **MAJOR OCEAN.**

YOU ARE HERE

GROWING OCEANS AND SHIFTING PLATES

By the late 1950s, the field of geology was really rocking! Geologists had most of the pieces they needed to explain how continents could move around the planet. They knew that the Earth was made up of layers and that the rocks below the crust could flow. They also saw that large mountain chains on land formed when two pieces of crust came crashing together. The one big problem that needed to be solved was explaining how the crust actually moved. This was answered by Harry Hess in 1962 with his idea of seafloor spreading.

Based on the maps made by Heezen and Tharp, Hess reasoned that the seafloor behaves like a giant conveyor belt. It turns out that the mid-ocean ridges have a string of active volcanoes running right down the middle of them. When new lava erupts at the ridges, it pushes the two sides of the ocean floor farther apart, making new oceanic crust as it does. Along the edge of the continents the old oceanic crust gets pushed back into the mantle. As the crust goes back down it begins to melt, creating magma that fuels volcanoes along the edges of the continents.

Plate Tectonics

OK, so where do we stand today when it comes to continental drift? Well, it turns out that Alfred Wegener was right when he said that the continents could move, but he was wrong in saying they moved through the crust. Instead, they move with the crust. About 50 years ago, a modern theory called plate tectonics explained this. Here's how it works:

As you know, the outermost layer of the Earth is the lithosphere, which is made up of about two dozen individual chunks called tectonic plates. These plates rest on top of the gooey asthenosphere layer. Some of the plates are made up of both oceanic and continental crust and others are just oceanic crust. Plate boundaries, the places where tectonic plates meet, are where most big earthquakes and active volcanoes occur because this is where the plates have the most movement. Magma that works its way up to the surface at mid-ocean ridges forms new oceanic crust and pushes the plates apart. Old oceanic crust is pushed back into the mantle at the trenches along the edges of the continents. When continents riding on top of the plates smash together they push the crust up, forming large mountain chains.

TECTONIC PLATES OF THE EARTH

THIS MAP SHOWS THE MAJOR TECTONIC PLATES THAT MAKE UP THE EARTH'S CRUST. THE ARROWS SHOW IN WHICH DIRECTION THE DIFFERENT PLATES ARE MOVING.

NEW CRUST FORMS AT THE MID-OCEAN RIDGES, PUSHING THE PLATES APART.

OLD OCEAN CRUST GETS PUSHED BACK DOWN INTO THE MANTLE, WHERE IT MELTS.

Pacific plate

Filipino plate

Australian plate

Antarctic plate

Eurasian plate

Indian plate

Arabian plate

African plate

North American plate

Caribbean plate

South American plate

Cocos plate

Nazca plate

Easter plate

Juan Fernandez plate

Juan de fuca plate

Pacific plate

DIRTMEISTER'S NUGGET

NOT ALL SPREADING HAPPENS IN THE OCEAN. THE RIFT VALLEY IN EAST AFRICA IS IN THE MIDDLE OF A CONTINENT. MOST GEOLOGISTS THINK THAT IN A FEW MILLION YEARS THIS WILL LEAD TO A NEW OCEAN IN THE MIDDLE OF AFRICA.

WOW! THIS BEATS SAILING IN A BOAT ANY DAY.

METAMORPHIC ROCKS AND THE BIG SQUEEZE

You can see evidence of plate tectonic activity from the distant past if you know how to read the rocks. One of the best ways to learn about ancient plate tectonic activity is to look for metamorphic rocks. These rocks have gone through big changes because they have been seriously cooked and crunched over time. This type of change usually happens when the rocks are deep underground where pressures are enormous. The reason we find them at the surface today is due to the fact that the rocks above them have been worn away.

There are a few different ways that a metamorphic rock can form. When hot magma rises up through the crust,

> Metamorphic rocks form from other rocks that have been heated and squeezed.

it can heat the rocks that surround it, causing new minerals to form. This type of change is called contact metamorphism.

In places such as faults, rocks often grind against each other with such force that it can also make them change. This is an example of dynamic metamorphism.

Metamorphic activity can also happen on a much larger scale when continents collide. In this case, rocks that are deeply buried get folded and twisted and often look as if they have been squeezed out of a tube, like toothpaste. Rocks that have their minerals stretched and lined up because of pressure coming from a certain direction are called foliated rocks.

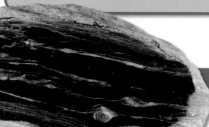

THIS PIECE OF MYLONITE FORMED IN A FAULT WHERE TWO PIECES OF CRUST SQUEEZED IT TOGETHER.

THIS PHYLLITE FORMED WHEN HEAT AND PRESSURE INSIDE THE EARTH CHANGED THE MINERALS IN THE ORIGINAL ROCK.

THIS PIECE OF GNEISS (PRONOUNCED "NICE") FORMED DURING LARGE-SCALE METAMORPHISM.

THIS GARNET SCHIST FORMED UNDER INTENSE METAMORPHISM.

MARBLE, A NON-FOLIATED ROCK, IS FORMED THROUGH THE METAMORPHISM OF LIMESTONE.

NOT ALL METAMORPHISM HAPPENS INSIDE THE PLANET. IMPACT METAMORPHISM HAPPENS TO ROCKS ON THE EARTH'S SURFACE WHEN A LARGE METEORITE SLAMS INTO THE GROUND. IMPACT METAMORPHISM IS RARE ON THE EARTH BECAUSE OUR ATMOSPHERE PROTECTS US FROM MOST METEORITES, BUT IT IS VERY COMMON ON THE MOON, MARS, AND MERCURY.

HEADS-UP, DIGGER! YOU DON'T WANT TO BECOME PART OF A CRATER!

QUARTZITE IS FORMED WHEN SANDSTONE IS SUBJECTED TO HIGH TEMPERATURES AND PRESSURE DEEP WITHIN THE EARTH'S CRUST.

CHAPTER 6

WHAT GOES UP MUST COME DOWN

WHAT'S SO GRAND ABOUT THE GRAND CANYON?

68

WEATHERING AWAY

The Grand Canyon didn't get to be so grand by accident! Rocks may seem like tough stuff, but over time they can be worn down by things like water, wind, snow, ice, and even plants. This process is called **weathering.** There are two main types of weathering.

The first type is called **physical** weathering and it's when large rocks break into smaller pieces. This is similar to hitting a rock with a sledgehammer. Here, the main change to the rock is size.

Of course, Mother Nature doesn't use sledgehammers to break rocks. But she does have some really cool chisels! When water seeps into the cracks in rocks and then freezes, the ice expands and splits the rock apart. This process is called **frost wedging.** See the experiment below.

Cracking, splitting, and smashing are not the only ways to weather rocks! Rocks can also be broken down by certain substances that are found in the environment. This is called **chemical weathering** and it also involves water, only this time the water stays liquid.

When water flows over rocks it reacts with minerals found on the surface, causing them to chemically change. You can see how this works by stirring a teaspoon of salt into a glass of water. The salt crystals quickly dissolve. Of course, not all minerals react to water as quickly as salt does, but over time water can cause enough chemical changes in minerals that eventually they fall apart. When water mixes with chemicals in the air and soil, it forms acids that also break down rock.

Technically speaking there is a third form of weathering, called **biological** weathering, and it happens when living things help to break down rocks. When tree roots grow down into the cracks in a rock, they can split it apart. This would be a case of **biophysical** weathering.

Biochemical weathering, another type, happens when living things produce chemicals that dissolve the minerals in rocks. Many mosses and lichens get the nutrients that they need to grow directly from rocks by using chemicals in their tissue to break the minerals down.

TRY THIS! 🧪 THE BIG CHILL

WHAT YOU'LL NEED

A small plastic water or soda bottle with a tight-fitting cap
A freezer

WHAT YOU'LL DO

Fill the bottle completely to the top with water and close tightly. Place the bottle in the freezer and let it sit for at least four hours. When you take the bottle out you will see that the water inside has turned to ice, and the bottle may have split open. What happened: When liquid water turns to ice it becomes as solid as a rock. Over time, repeated cycles of freezing and thawing can easily split even the hardest rock!

These mountain peaks in Navarre, Spain, formed as the rocks slowly weathered away.

WHEN SALT CRYSTALS GROW IN TINY CRACKS IN ROCKS, THEY CAN DO THE SAME THING AS ICE. THIS HAPPENS A LOT TO ROCKS NEAR THE OCEAN, WHERE THERE IS A LOT OF SALT SPRAY.

Tree roots growing into rocks are a form of bio-physical weathering.

The lichens covering this rock are breaking it down using biochemical weathering.

CAREFUL, DIGGER, DON'T CLOBBER THE CRAB INSTEAD OF THE ROCK!

This boulder has been split by ice growing in the cracks over time. It is an example of frost wedging.

71

SLIP SLIDING AWAY

After rocks have been beaten, bashed, and broken down by weathering, the smaller pieces that are left behind are called **sediment.** At this point the force of gravity takes over and the sediment begins to move. This is called **erosion.**

If the pieces of sediment are small enough, wind and water can pick them up and carry them away. Erosion can also be caused by gravity alone when events like rock falls, avalanches, slides, and slumps happen.

Rock falls and slides usually happen on really steep cliffs. As rocks on the top of the cliff start to weather they lose their strength and eventually come crashing down.

Unlike a slide, which usually happens on cliffs with large blocks of rocks, a slump usually happens in areas that have thick piles of loose sediment. You've probably experienced slumping of sediment if you have ever built a sand castle at the beach and tried to make it a bit too tall.

Gravity is the main force that causes erosion in rocks.

Being crushed under a pile of falling rocks is bad, but getting caught in a debris flow can be even worse. Like slumps, these usually happen along hills that are made of thick piles of sediment. After a heavy rain (or lots of melting snow), water seeps into the sediment and turns it into a slippery, muddy mass that starts flowing downhill, burying everything in its path.

One of the most important jobs that a geologist can do is to identify places where ancient falls, flows, and slides have occurred, because history usually repeats itself. The area of geology that analyzes the land surface is called **geomorphology,** which basically means "the shape of the Earth."

Rock slides like this one in California often happen along steep cliffs.

When sediments get soaked, mudslides can bury roads or houses.

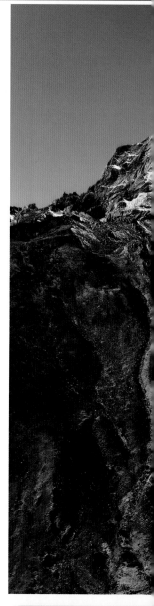

OVER TIME, EVEN THE TALLEST MOUNTAINS GET WORN DOWN BY EROSION.

BIO FLORENCE BASCOM FIRST WOMAN OF AMERICAN GEOLOGY

BIRTHPLACE: UNITED STATES BIRTH YEAR: 1862

Florence Bascom liked to break new ground and made a habit of being the first woman to do many things. Florence became interested in geology at a young age after taking several trips with her father and observing many natural landscapes. After getting a master's degree in geology, Florence went on to be the first woman to get a Ph.D. from Johns Hopkins University.

In 1895, Bascom began teaching at Bryn Mawr College, and even though she loved to teach she also wanted to get out into the field and actually do geology! In 1896, she finally got her wish and was named the first woman geologist to ever work for the United States Geological Survey. For the next 40 years she worked as a geologist, specializing in geomorphology and mineralogy while continuing to teach. Along the way she also became the first woman to present a paper to the Geological Society in Washington, D.C., and the first woman member of the Geological Society of America, opening the door for the other women geologists who followed her.

WELL, BLOW ME DOWN

Gravity isn't the only thing that causes rocks to come crashing down to Earth! In places that are very dry, **wind** can cause massive amounts of erosion. If you don't think that the wind can wear things down, just visit a sandy beach on a windy day. It can be a painful experience!

Wind erosion is especially powerful in dry environments because there are very few plants growing in these areas. Grasses and other plants keep sediment from blowing away by giving it a protective cover. Plant roots help grab on to the sediment, making it hard for wind or water to move it, and tall plants act like natural "wind breaks," blocking the flow of air so the wind is not as powerful.

On windy days, sand, silt, and clay can easily be picked up and carried many miles. During the famous Dust Bowl of the 1930s, for example, large windstorms blowing across the middle of the United States carried huge clouds of sediment hundreds of miles, making it almost impossible for people to see and breathe.

The raw power of blowing sediment can also do a serious job of shaping the rocks. Sand grains that fly through the air can wear away the surface of rocks, making them look really weird. Geologists call these sandblasted rocks **ventifacts.** Most ventifacts have a polished surface and in some cases they will be curved and shaped almost as if a sculptor had been working on them.

> Ventifacts are rocks that have been shaped by wind erosion.

If conditions are just right, high winds can also move some pretty large stones across the desert floor. Such is the case of the mysterious "sailing stones" found in a place called Racetrack Playa, in Death Valley National Park. The area has a large, flat lake bed that is dry most of the time. Every so often you find a large stone that has a long trail behind it.

Now when I say that these rocks are large, I'm not joking around. Some weigh several hundred pounds, so most people wouldn't be able to budge them. To make the mystery even more complex, there are no tire tracks, tread marks, or footprints anywhere near them.

For the longest time the rocks had people wondering. What made them move? Was it some guy training for a Strongest Man competition, or maybe the government was testing out a new secret weapon? Or maybe it was aliens from space! After years of studying the situation, geologists think they have the answer. Here's the scoop ...

It doesn't rain much in Death Valley, but when it does, the lake fills up with a thin layer of water, which often freezes at night. During the day it gets warm and the ice breaks up into large sheets. Studies have shown that gusts of wind are strong enough to get some of these ice sheets moving. When the sheets push against the rocks, it makes them slide on the muddy bottom, leaving the trails behind them.

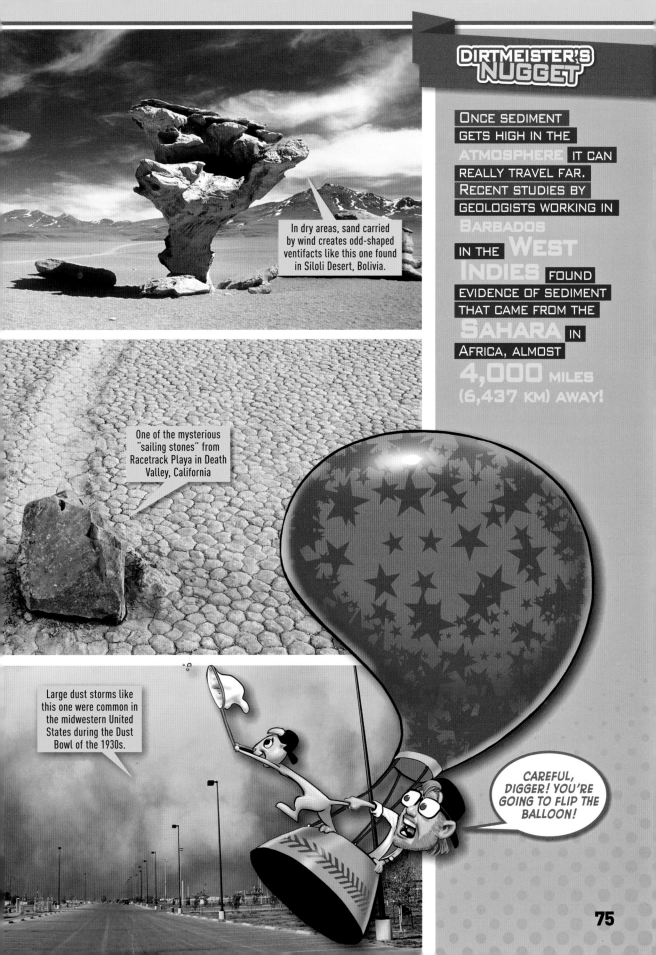

In dry areas, sand carried by wind creates odd-shaped ventifacts like this one found in Siloli Desert, Bolivia.

ONCE SEDIMENT GETS HIGH IN THE ATMOSPHERE IT CAN REALLY TRAVEL FAR. RECENT STUDIES BY GEOLOGISTS WORKING IN BARBADOS IN THE WEST INDIES FOUND EVIDENCE OF SEDIMENT THAT CAME FROM THE SAHARA IN AFRICA, ALMOST 4,000 MILES (6,437 KM) AWAY!

One of the mysterious "sailing stones" from Racetrack Playa in Death Valley, California

Large dust storms like this one were common in the midwestern United States during the Dust Bowl of the 1930s.

CAREFUL, DIGGER! YOU'RE GOING TO FLIP THE BALLOON!

ICE IS NICE

So how does moving ice shape the surface of the Earth? It's all about **glaciers!** A glacier is a large mass of ice that forms on the land because of the steady buildup of snow in cold areas. Glaciers usually take decades to form. Eventually enough snow builds up so that the pressure on the bottom of the pile causes it to change to ice. The ice then begins to flow downhill under the force of gravity, just like a slow-moving river.

> Glaciers are like slow-moving rivers of ice that flow due to gravity.

There are two main types of glaciers. **Mountain glaciers** form at the tops of tall mountains above the **snow line.** The snow line is the elevation on a mountain above which the snow never melts, even in the summer. Mountain glaciers usually follow the path of an existing valley. As the glacier flows, it scrapes its way along the bottom and sides, picking up and carrying any loose rock and sediment with it, making the valley wider and deeper as it goes. Don't think of a glacier as a bulldozer, though. It doesn't push the sediment in front of it. Instead it is more like a conveyor belt, trapping sediment inside of it and carrying big boulders on top of it. As long as it keeps snowing at the back end of the glacier, the glacier will keep moving forward.

CONTINENTAL ICE SHEETS

In places such as Antarctica and Greenland, gigantic glaciers form and cover much of the land surface. These enormous glaciers are called **continental ice sheets.**

Continental ice sheets also move, but when they do they spread out in all directions from a central point where the snow builds up. Ice sheets can be miles thick, burying hills and small mountains. Eventually they reach the ocean, where they begin to break up. Geologists call this process calving. **Calving** is how icebergs form.

Right now continental ice sheets are melting at an alarming rate and many scientists believe that this is due to global warming. About 13,000 years ago, mammoth ice sheets covered a large part of the Northern Hemisphere. And today, some climate scientists believe that in a few hundred years many of Earth's glaciers will be gone.

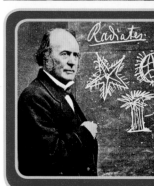

When Alsek Glacier in Alaska reaches the ocean it breaks up by a process called calving, forming icebergs.

HEY, YOU GUYS AREN'T SUPPOSED TO BE UP HERE!

BIO LOUIS AGASSIZ THE ICE MAN COMETH

BIRTHPLACE: SWITZERLAND   BIRTH YEAR: 1807

Louis Agassiz earned both a Ph.D. and M.D. before he moved to Paris and began to study glaciers.

Agassiz was convinced that in the past, large continent-size glaciers had covered much of northern Europe and North America. He set up a hut on top of an active valley glacier, and he spent years tracking the movements of the ice and surveying the region. He noticed that glaciers could carry giant boulders many miles. And as the glaciers flowed, they often left deep grooves on the bedrock, pointing the way from which they came.

Because of his groundbreaking work, Louis Agassiz is regarded as one of the most influential people in the area of natural science, and he is the main reason that we know about the ice ages today!

CARVING OUT A CANYON

We've seen how weathering can break down hard rocks and how gravity, wind, and ice can transport the broken bits of sediment away. Now it's time to put the pieces together to see how these factors all helped carve out the Grand Canyon.

The Grand Canyon is a deep valley located in the northwestern part of Arizona. In places, the Grand Canyon is over a mile deep and more than 18 miles (29 km) wide. In total, it stretches over 275 miles (443 km). At the bottom of the Grand Canyon is the Colorado River, which gets its start from melting snow in the Rocky Mountains of Colorado to the east and then flows southwest to Mexico.

Geologists still aren't sure when the Grand Canyon started forming. What we do know is that sometime in the past, tectonic forces began to push this area up. Remember what tectonic forces are? They happen when continental plates start pushing together. This lifting made the Colorado River flow faster, giving it more energy to cut through the underlying rock.

Rivers and streams can do a lot of erosion if the water is moving fast enough. The force of the flowing water picks up small pieces of loose rock and pushes them along the river bottom. Smaller sediment that is carried by the water also scours the bottom of the river, just like sandpaper rubbing on wood.

Most of the erosion that happens because of rivers is something called **downcutting.** The river cuts a narrow channel (or path) down through the underlying rock, carrying away the loose particles of rock and sediments. As long as the water keeps moving fast, or if there are floods every so often, then the stream can cut deeper into the rock.

While the downcutting of the Colorado River explains why the canyon is so deep, it does not explain how it got to be so wide. That's caused by other types of weathering and erosion. During the winter and at night it can get quite cold in this part of the country, so frost wedging helps break up the rocks along the edges of the canyon. The area is also very dry so there are not many plants. This means that the wind can easily remove some of the smaller pieces of sediment from the top of the canyon. As the walls get steeper, rocks near the top of the canyon fall and slide into the river below, where they get broken up and carried away. And that, my friends, is why the Grand Canyon is so grand.

> The rocks at the bottom of the Grand Canyon are over one billion years old!

The Grand Canyon stretches over 275 miles (443 km), starting at Arizona's northern border with Utah and going almost to the Nevada border in the west.

GEOLOGISTS STILL AREN'T SURE WHEN THE GRAND CANYON STARTED FORMING. MOST THINK THAT IT IS ONLY ABOUT 6 MILLION YEARS OLD BUT SOME RECENT STUDIES SUGGEST THAT IT MAY HAVE FIRST BEGUN FORMING AROUND 70 MILLION YEARS AGO!

LOOK, DIGGER! THE SAND IS MAKING LAYERS, JUST LIKE IN THE GRAND CANYON.

THE ROCK CYCLE
LOOK-ALIKE ROCKS

LITTLE GRAINS LEAD TO BIG DEPOSITS

We just learned that with the process of weathering, rocks are smashed and bashed into pieces of sediment. But what happens next? That's when water, wind, and glaciers all do their transport thing.

Eventually all of the sediments transported by wind, water, and ice stop moving and start to pile up, forming different types of sedimentary deposits. The type of deposits that form from windblown sediment looks very different from the deposits created by either glaciers or rivers. Wind usually deposits sediment in even layers and often forms large sloping piles called dunes.

Glaciers are the exact opposite of wind. Because ice is pretty solid stuff, glaciers usually transport a big mix of different-size sediment. When the ice finally melts, the mixed sediment gets dumped in place.

Streams can deposit sediment anywhere along the valley through which they flow. When the flowing water meets a lake or the ocean it slows down so much that it can no longer carry sediment. When this happens, the sediment begins to pile up at the mouth of the river or stream, forming something called a delta. A delta is a large pile of sediment that over time can actually block the flow of the river that created it.

A little less than 100 years ago, looking at sediments was pretty much guesswork. These days, however, scientists use a special scale to separate sediments based on the size of the pieces.

Wind can only carry small pieces of sediment, which can be deposited into big piles called dunes.

After glaciers melt, they often create piles of mixed-size sediments called moraines.

BIO CHESTER KEELER WENTWORTH MEASUREMENT MAN

BIRTHPLACE: UNITED STATES   BIRTH YEAR: 1891

Most people think of sand as the stuff you dig in at the beach, but to a geologist it has a special meaning. The words "sand," "silt," and even "boulder" are used to describe the size of sediments. These terms really didn't have a scientific meaning until Chester Wentworth came along.

Wentworth got his start measuring sediment as a college student. In 1922, he published a paper with terms for classification, and the Wentworth grain size scale was born.

Over the next 40 years Wentworth had a long and distinguished career working as a geologist, and today his scale is used by geologists and soil scientists all over the world to describe sediments.

THIS SATELLITE IMAGE SHOWS HOW THE MISSISSIPPI RIVER BUILDS AN ENORMOUS PILE OF SEDIMENT, CALLED A DELTA, WHERE IT ENTERS THE GULF OF MEXICO.

WENTWORTH SCALE OF ROCK PARTICLE SIZES

PARTICLE SIZE	CLASSIFICATION
BOULDER	Above 256 mm
COBBLE	64–256 mm
PEBBLE	4–64 mm
GRAVEL	2–4 mm
VERY COARSE SAND	1–2 mm
COARSE SAND	0.5–1 mm
MEDIUM SAND	0.25–0.5 mm
FINE SAND	0.125–0.25 mm
VERY FINE SAND	0.062–0.125 mm
SILT	0.004–0.062 mm
CLAY	Less than 0.004 mm

WHICH WAY IS UP?
SEDIMENTARY ENVIRONMENTS AND STRUCTURES

Geologists love to dig in the dirt! By studying the way that sediments are deposited today, they can go back and look at ancient sedimentary deposits and figure out the environment in which they formed.

Whenever sediments get deposited, they form features called **sedimentary structures.** Sedimentary structures help geologists figure out if the sediments were moved by water, wind, or something else. They can also figure out which direction the sediments came from, and even what the climate was like.

Let's say that there is a small, slow-moving stream emptying into a lake. Because the water is moving slowly, the sediment that it deposits would be fine-grain sand, silt, and clay. Now imagine that there is a huge rainstorm upstream and all of a sudden the little stream becomes a raging river. The flood of water is now carrying coarse sand, gravel, and pebbles. Eventually the water slows down again and these large sediments are deposited on top of the fine sand below. Once the stream goes back to normal, a new layer of fine sediment is deposited on top of the big pieces and the cycle continues. This change in the size of the sediment that you see is a type of sedimentary structure called a **graded bed.**

Geologists use changes in sediment size to mark different layers in the rock. Each of these layers is called a bed.

BIO NICOLAUS STENO ROCKING THROUGH TIME

BIRTHPLACE: DENMARK   BIRTH YEAR: 1638

Nicolaus Steno was one talented dude! In addition to being one of the founding fathers of modern geology, he was also an important physician and religious leader.

After doing his early studies in Copenhagen, he moved to Amsterdam and then to Italy, where he conducted research on human anatomy, making several important discoveries in biology. Then he turned his attention to the Earth.

Steno began studying the rocks of Italy and realized that the different rock layers (which we now call **strata**) preserved a record of geological events that had happened in the past. In 1669, he published a book outlining his geological findings. Today these observations have become known as Steno's laws and they form the groundwork for the modern science of strata, called **stratigraphy.**

LAYERS OF DIFFERENT STRATA ARE CLEARLY VISIBLE IN THESE CLIFFS AT THE GRAND STAIRCASE-ESCALANTE NATIONAL MONUMENT IN UTAH.

IF YOU HAVE EVER SPENT TIME IN THE **SHALLOW WATER** OF A LAKE OR A SLOW-MOVING RIVER WITH **A SANDY BOTTOM,** YOU'VE PROBABLY NOTICED THAT THE BOTTOM HAS LITTLE **BUMPS IN IT.** THESE ARE CALLED **RIPPLE MARKS.** WHEN GEOLOGISTS FIND RIPPLE MARKS IN **SEDIMENTARY ROCKS** IT TELLS THEM THE DIRECTION THAT THE WATER FLOWED AND ALSO GIVES SOME CLUES ABOUT **HOW DEEP THE WATER WAS.**

LOOK HERE, DIGGER, YOU CAN SEE THE LITTLE RIPPLE MARKS THAT THE WATER MADE IN THE SAND!

GETTING STUCK ON SEDIMENTS

Sediments don't stay soft and mushy forever. If the conditions are right, loose sediment often gets changed into solid rock. Geologists call this **lithification,** and it's a slow process during which the sediments go through many different changes.

The first type of change usually happens when sediments get squeezed together. As new layers get added to the top of the pile the older layers on the bottom get squished together. This makes the spaces between the grains smaller and pushes out much of the water that was trapped in the sediment.

Squeezing sediments together can only take you so far when it comes to making a rock. There is often a second type of change in which the pieces of sediment actually get stuck together. This happens when some type of chemical substance fills in the spaces between the grains and acts like cement, gluing the particles together. You can see how this happens by trying a simple experiment, but you are going to have to wait about three days to get the final result!

> Lithification is a process in which soft sediments get turned back into solid rocks again.

THIS ROCK IS CALLED A CONGLOMERATE. IT IS MADE UP OF MANY SMALLER ROCKS THAT HAVE BEEN CEMENTED TOGETHER.

TRY THIS! 🧪 DESIGN A ROCK

WHAT YOU'LL NEED

A small (3 oz) disposable plastic cup
A bottle of white glue
Some dry sand and pebbles

WHAT YOU'LL DO

Start by filling the bottom of the cup with a thick layer of glue. Next add some sand and pebbles so the cup is about three-quarters full. Slowly pour some more glue on top of the sediment and watch how it starts to flow down between the grains. Once the glue has settled, place the cup in a location where it will not be disturbed and allow it to rest for at least three days. After at least three days have passed, check to see if the glue has hardened by gently squeezing the sides of the cup. If the sides of the cup feel squishy, or if any liquid glue is still visible, let the cup sit for another day or two. If the sediment in the cup feels hard then gently peel away the cup and presto! You'll have your very own sedimentary rock.

WHEN SEDIMENT GETS PILED UP, THE LAYERS NEAR THE BOTTOM GET COMPACTED OR SQUEEZED TOGETHER.

DIRTMEISTER'S NUGGET

IN ADDITION TO THE PILING ON OF NEW SEDIMENTS, COMPACTION CAN ALSO TAKE PLACE IN OLDER LAYERS OF SEDIMENT BECAUSE OF VIBRATIONS IN THE GROUND. SOME GEOLOGISTS CALL THIS THE "CORN FLAKE EFFECT" BECAUSE IT OFTEN HAPPENS IN CEREAL BOXES.

HEY, DIGGER, IF YOU FIND A PRIZE AT THE BOTTOM OF THE BOX, IT'S MINE!

THE NITTY GRITTY OF SEDIMENTARY ROCKS

Weathering makes lots of different sediments. So that means there are many types of **sedimentary** rocks! Geologists usually divide sedimentary rocks into three different groups based on the way they come together.

First, there are the rocks with pieces of other rocks that have been squeezed or glued together. They include some of the most common rocks such as sandstone, shale, and conglomerate. The main difference between these three rocks is the size of the sediment that they are made from. A **conglomerate** has big chunks of rocks while shale is made from tiny pieces of clay. Can you guess what sandstone is made from?

The second group of sedimentary rocks is made from the **shells** of sea creatures such as clams and corals. When these creatures die, their shells sink to the bottom. In shallow areas where there are lots of waves, the shells usually get smashed into smaller pieces but in the deep water, the shells turn into a gooey layer on the bottom.

As the water moves the ooze around, it will sometimes make little balls of lime called ooliths that sort of look like little eyeballs in the rock! Most of the time the mud just hardens and forms a rock called **limestone.**

Do you like salt on your French fries? If so, you can thank the last type of sedimentary rock, called an **evaporite,** for that bit of flavor. One of the most common evaporites is our old friend halite, or table salt. When water dissolves rocks, many of the chemicals hang out in the water. That's why ocean water tastes salty. When pools of salt water start to dry out, or evaporate, the chemicals get left behind and form crystals.

You can easily see this for yourself by taking a few spoons of salt and dissolving it in a cup of water. Stick the cup in a safe place for a few days. When you come back you will see that the water is gone and the inside of the cup will have little white salt crystals attached to it.

THIS LIMESTONE CAME FROM THE SHELLS OF SEA CREATURES THAT DISSOLVED AND FORMED A NEW ROCK.

THIS SHALE IS MADE FROM LAYERS OF FINE MUD THAT WERE SQUEEZED BACK TOGETHER.

THIS GYPSUM FORMED WHEN MINERAL-RICH WATER EVAPORATED, LEAVING THE CRYSTALS BEHIND.

THIS SANDSTONE IS MADE FROM SAND GRAINS THAT WERE CEMENTED TOGETHER.

ANTELOPE CANYON NEAR PAGE, ARIZONA, IS MADE FROM SEDIMENTARY ROCKS THAT HAVE ERODED OVER TIME.

THE NATURAL CHALK THAT PEOPLE FIRST USED FOR DRAWING IS A SEDIMENTARY ROCK MADE FROM TINY SEA CREATURES CALLED COCCOLITHS. IN ENGLAND THERE ARE GIANT CLIFFS MADE OF CHALK, CALLED THE WHITE CLIFFS OF DOVER.

The famous White Cliffs of Dover in England are made of chalk!

VERY FUNNY, DIGGER. SO NOW YOU THINK YOU'RE AN ARTIST?

THE ROCK CYCLE

Since sedimentary rocks are basically recycled rocks, the question is, how many different ways can rocks be changed to make new rocks? Well, the answer is *a lot!* Here on Earth, we don't have very many really old rocks. That's because processes such as weathering, erosion, volcanism, and plate tectonics are constantly destroying the old rocks and using the chemicals in them to make new rocks. Geologists call this never-ending series of changes the rock cycle.

HERE'S HOW IT WORKS:

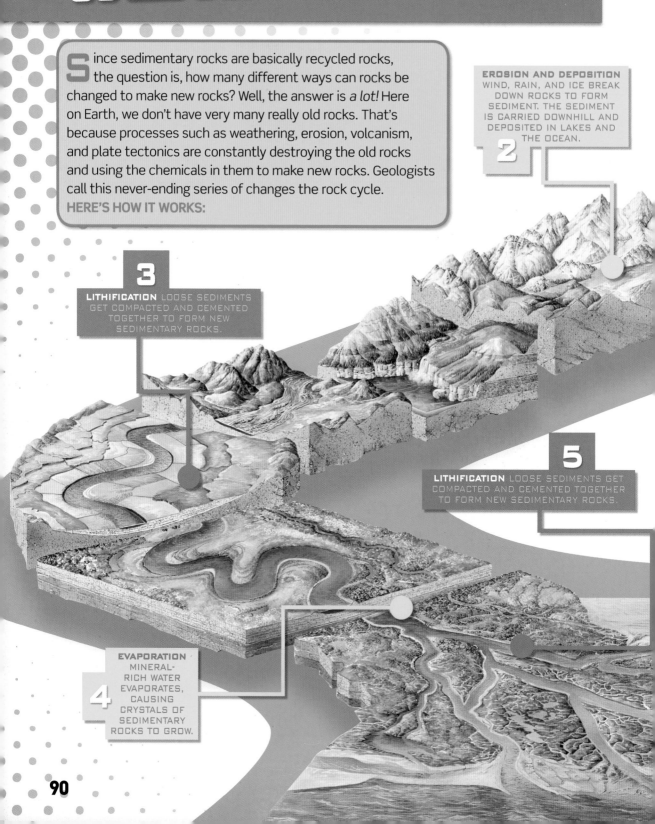

EROSION AND DEPOSITION WIND, RAIN, AND ICE BREAK DOWN ROCKS TO FORM SEDIMENT. THE SEDIMENT IS CARRIED DOWNHILL AND DEPOSITED IN LAKES AND THE OCEAN.

2

3

LITHIFICATION LOOSE SEDIMENTS GET COMPACTED AND CEMENTED TOGETHER TO FORM NEW SEDIMENTARY ROCKS.

5

LITHIFICATION LOOSE SEDIMENTS GET COMPACTED AND CEMENTED TOGETHER TO FORM NEW SEDIMENTARY ROCKS.

4

EVAPORATION MINERAL-RICH WATER EVAPORATES, CAUSING CRYSTALS OF SEDIMENTARY ROCKS TO GROW.

1

MAGMA UNDERGROUND HEAT CAUSES MINERALS TO MELT TO FORM MAGMA. SOME OF THIS MAGMA MOVES TO THE SURFACE TO FORM LAVA, AND SOME COOLS IN PLACE TO FORM NEW INTRUSIVE ROCKS.

WELL, I THINK THAT WE'VE COVERED JUST ABOUT ALL THE WAYS THAT **ROCKS** CAN BE **RECYCLED** INTO OTHER ROCKS! THE BOTTOM LINE IS THAT MOST ROCKS THAT WE FIND ON THE SURFACE OF THE EARTH HAVE PROBABLY GONE THROUGH THE **ROCK CYCLE** MORE THAN JUST **A FEW TIMES.**

C'MON, DIGGER, WE'VE GOT DINOS WAITING FOR US!

VOLCANO NEW IGNEOUS ROCKS FORM FROM COOLED LAVA FLOWING OUT OF VOLCANOES AT THE EARTH'S SURFACE.

6

7

TECTONIC ACTION ROCKS FROM THE SURFACE GET BURIED AND PUSHED BACK INTO THE EARTH, WHERE THEY ARE HEATED AND SQUEEZED. THE MINERALS SLOWLY CHANGE TO FORM METAMORPHIC ROCKS.

CHAPTER 8

DIGGING OLD DEAD THINGS

WHAT HAPPENED TO THE DINOSAURS?

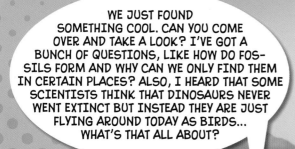

WHAT IS A FOSSIL?

Did you know that there are hundreds of different kinds of **fossils?** There are fossils of everything from dinosaur bones and footprints to shells and even ancient poop! One of the coolest fossils is an insect or some other small animal trapped in **amber.** Amber is formed from hardened tree sap. When bugs crawl through the sap, they get stuck and if more sap flows on top of them, they can be sealed inside. When the sap hardens you have a rock with a perfectly preserved insect inside.

Another type of fossil is a **mold,** which is really common in seashells. A mold forms when something hard is pushed down into some soft sediment. Over time it gets buried and the sediment turns into stone. The original shell will often dissolve away, leaving a perfect copy of the shell in the rock. Then, if the mold fills up with another type of sediment that hardens into rock, you have a cast, which is a near-perfect copy of the original shell.

> Fossils are the remains of living things that have been preserved.

Another way of forming fossils is by **permineralization.** This often happens with dinosaur bones when they get buried. Bones have lots of little holes in them. Water flowing through the sediment can fill these holes with new minerals. Sometimes geologists will say that the bone has become **petrified.** This doesn't mean that it is scared stiff—it has just turned to stone.

There is one final type of fossil—one that does not actually show the remains of the living thing itself but does help scientists figure out what a living thing looked like, how it moved, and what it ate. These are called **trace fossils.** Trace fossils include evidence such as trails and footprints. Scientists can use them to calculate how fast an animal moved or the type of environment in which it lived. One of the most important trace fossils is coprolite, which is a polite way of saying fossilized poop. Some coprolites even contain the remains of what the animal had for its last meal!

Scientists can use dinosaur footprints to calculate how big the animal was and how fast it moved.

Coprolite, or fossilized poop, can sometimes be used to tell what an animal ate.

THIS TINY LIZARD WAS TRAPPED IN SAP BEFORE IT DIED. AS THE SAP HARDENED IT FORMED A STONE CALLED AMBER, PERFECTLY PRESERVING THE LIZARD INSIDE.

SOMETIMES THE ORIGINAL REMAINS OF AN ANIMAL CAN BE REPLACED BY A NEW MINERAL, SUCH AS **PYRITE**, AFTER IT HAS BEEN BURIED IN THE GROUND. THIS PRODUCES A FOSSIL THAT LOOKS LIKE **IT IS MADE OF GOLD ... WELL, FOOL'S GOLD ANYWAY!**

DON'T BE FOOLED, DIGGER. THAT SHELL IS ONLY MADE OF PYRITE!

THIS FOSSIL IS A CAST OF A TRILOBITE, WHICH WAS A SEA CREATURE THAT RESEMBLES A MODERN-DAY INSECT.

THE FOSSIL LIMITS

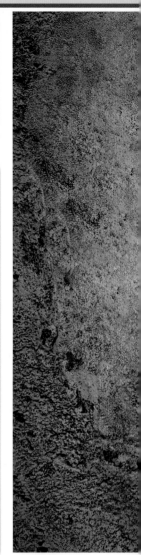

Finding the **fossils** of extinct critters or plants can solve many mysteries. Fossils can tell us how big a creature was, what it ate, and even how fast it ran. From plant fossils we get an idea of what the climate was like and possibly the position of the continents in the distant past.

Before a fossil can even form, the conditions have to be just right. When most animals and plants die, their remains immediately start to rot away, so in a few short weeks there is nothing left. For a fossil to form, the dead thing has to get buried in sediment very quickly. This is why there are very few fossils showing the soft parts of animals—it takes much longer for parts like bones and teeth to decompose, so they stand a better chance of being preserved than skin or hair.

When scientists find fossils, the real fun is just starting. Take the dinosaurs, for example. When **paleontologists** find them in the field they rarely look like they do in a museum. Many bones are broken or missing entirely and the bones are usually separated from each other. Often, when a dinosaur dies, it is not alone! There may be bones from several different individuals or species all jumbled together. It is like trying to put together a giant jigsaw puzzle, only you have pieces from other puzzles and some pieces are missing altogether—and you don't have a picture showing what the final thing should look like!

TRY THIS! 🧪 FIGURING OUT FOSSILS

WHAT YOU'LL NEED

A large lump of modeling clay
A seashell, a paper clip, a coin, a key, or some other small, hard objects

WHAT YOU'LL DO

Take the clay and split it into three or four equal-size pieces. Roll each piece into a ball and flatten it into a fat pancake. Carefully press each object into one of the clay pieces and remove it. You should now have an impression of each object in the clay. If these harden you will have created a mold. Place the mold next to the object that you used to make it and carefully observe the two. See how they are the same and how they are different. If you were to be given just the mold, would you be able to tell what it was? What pieces of information would be missing?

Can you tell the size or the color of the object? Can you see patterns on the surface? This gives you some idea of the guesswork involved in the work of paleontologists when studying and trying to identify fossils.

Finding a perfectly preserved skeleton with all the pieces in place is quite rare.

MOST FOSSILS ARE FOUND IN **SEDIMENTARY ROCKS** BUT THERE ARE SOME RARE EXCEPTIONS. SOMETIMES AN ANIMAL WILL GET BURIED IN **A LAYER OF ASH** FROM **AN ERUPTING VOLCANO** THAT ISN'T QUITE HOT ENOUGH TO DESTROY THE REMAINS. WHEN THE ASH HARDENS IT MAKES **AN AWESOME FOSSIL!**

CAREFUL, DIGGER, THOSE FOSSIL TEETH ARE SHARP.

Scientists carefully remove fossilized bone from rock while working at a dig site of a fossilized dinosaur at Dinosaur Provincial Park, Alberta, Canada.

97

INDEX FOSSILS AND AGE DATING

As scientists found more fossils, they realized that fossils could help them figure out the age of rocks in different locations around the world.

Let's say that you are a geologist working in New York and there is a certain type of fossil in the rocks that you are studying. A friend of yours is also a geologist, but she is working across the Atlantic Ocean in Germany. She finds the exact same fossil in her rocks. The fact that the rocks that each of you are studying have the same fossil in them suggests that the rocks are about the same age. Fossils that can be found in rocks in many places around the world are called **index fossils.** Index fossils allow geologists to link up the ages of rocks from all over the world. The best index fossils are from animals and plants that lived for only a short time.

Geologists use index fossils to travel back in time. In most cases they will use a collection of different fossils that all came from the same time period to match rocks. This reduces the chance of making a mistake when they try to figure out which rocks came first. The process of matching strata from different areas is called cross-correlation and it's kind of like a puzzle.

In the early 1800s, scientists working in Europe had already used these age-dating techniques to build a time line. At the same time in England, a group of fossil hunters started making remarkable finds, including the bones from a group of large creatures. They didn't know it at the time, but what they found were some of the first dinosaur fossils!

A plesiosaur was a long-necked carnivorous reptile. The first one was discovered by Mary Anning. These beasts lived in the seas of the Mesozoic era from 230 to 65 million years ago.

BIO MARY ANNING Fossilist Extraordinaire

BIRTHPLACE: ENGLAND   BIRTH YEAR: 1799

Long before there were paleontologists there was a group of fossil hunters called fossilists. One of the best was Mary Anning. As a child, Mary would often walk the beach with her father, and she became quite good at spotting tiny pieces of fossils sticking out of the ground. One day, when she was about 11 years old, she and her brother spotted what he thought was the tip of a crocodile skull. Mary spent the next few months chipping the skull out of the rock. What she discovered was an almost entirely intact skeleton of a giant marine reptile called an ichthyosaur.

Over the next 30 years, Mary Anning made many other discoveries, including the first known plesiosaur. Even though she didn't have any formal schooling, Anning became an expert, and many of the top paleontologists consulted her on their work.

TRILOBITES OFTEN MAKE GOOD INDEX FOSSILS BECAUSE THEY ARE FOUND IN MANY LOCATIONS IN THE WORLD.

THE TERM "DINOSAUR" WAS FIRST USED BY THE ENGLISH SCIENTIST RICHARD OWEN IN 1841 TO DESCRIBE A GROUP OF RELATED FOSSILS THAT MOST PEOPLE WERE SIMPLY CALLING DRAGONS. THE WORD "DINOSAUR" COMES FROM TWO GREEK WORDS THAT MEAN "TERRIBLE LIZARD."

NICE MASK, DIGGER. YOU LOOK JUST LIKE A MINI T. REX!

THE FOSSIL RECORD AND EVOLUTION

By the early 1800s, new fossils were being discovered almost every day. This showed that Earth was once home to many strange life-forms. At the time, most people were firm believers in the idea that the Earth was only a few thousand years old. Scientists were trying hard to make these new discoveries fit in with the old ideas, but it was becoming more difficult.

In the mid-1800s, an English naturalist named Charles Darwin came up with a theory to explain how animals and plants could slowly change over time. He called his theory **natural selection.** The way natural selection works is pretty simple. For animals to survive they must compete for basic needs such as food, water, shelter, and air. As populations grow or as the environment changes, there is more competition and only those individuals that have the ability to get and use the resources they need will survive. You may have heard this part of it explained by the term "survival of the fittest." Those animals that do survive will pass those natural abilities (biologists call them traits) to their offspring. After many generations of this happening, the species itself will change or **evolve.**

Today the theory of evolution is supported by what scientists find in fossils. The most important key to making evolution work is time. A species usually needs hundreds if not thousands of years for these changes to take place.

Natural selection is usually explained as survival of the fittest.

A QUICK WORD ABOUT THE WORD "THEORY"

Despite all the evidence from fossils and DNA testing, many people still do not believe that evolution is possible. One of the major complaints they have is that evolution is just a theory and that theories are not facts or scientific laws. While it is true that evolution is considered a theory, there are hard facts to support it.

Much of the confusion comes from the way that scientists use the word "theory." A scientific theory is not simply an educated guess. That would be what scientists call a hypothesis. Before something can be considered a scientific theory, the people who present it lay out arguments showing all the facts they have to support it. Next, the potential theory has to be checked by other scientists. Only after the theory has been tested over and over again, and revisions are made, is it released. The important thing with any theory is to get as many facts as you can on both sides of the argument and then make up your own mind!

ANGIOSPERMS

FERNS

VERTEBRATES

GYMNOSPERMS

UROCHORDATES

ARTHROPODS

ECHINODERMS

ASCOBOLUS

NEMATODES

MOLLUSKS

NEUROSPORA

COELENTERATES

GREEN ALGAE

SLIME MOLDS

SPONGES

AMOEBAE

DIATOMS

HELIOZOANS

YEASTS

BROWN
ALGAE

CILATES

RED ALGAE

ARCHAEBACTERIA

DINOFLAGELLATES

PURPLE BACTERIA

CYANOBACTERIA

MYXOBACTERIA

GRAM POSITIVE BACTERIA

CHARLES DARWIN PRESENTED HIS THEORY OF EVOLUTION IN 1859 IN A BOOK CALLED **ORIGIN OF SPECIES.** SINCE THEN, THOUSANDS OF SCIENTISTS HAVE REVIEWED IT, AND APART FROM A FEW SMALL CHANGES, IT HAS STOOD THE TEST OF TIME. IN FACT IF ANYTHING, **NEW EVIDENCE** FROM RECENTLY DISCOVERED DINOSAUR FOSSILS SEEMS TO MAKE THE **THEORY EVEN STRONGER.**

GET A GOOD CLOSE-UP SHOT OF ME AND MY DISTANT COUSIN, DIGGER!

101

THE DEMISE OF THE DINOS

Even though some cockroaches seem to live forever, every single species of animal or plant, including us humans, will probably become **extinct.** When an animal or plant becomes extinct, it basically means that there are no more living members of that species alive on the planet. Most often, when a species becomes extinct it is due to some sort of environmental change. Extinctions can be caused by the climate getting too cold or too dry. Or it could be the result of an animal losing its only food source. Extinctions usually happen slowly, affecting only a few species at a time. That's why what happened to the dinosaurs is so startling. When they died out it wasn't just a few species, it was virtually all of them.

> In a mass extinction, many different animals and plants all die out at once.

Whatever caused their extinction didn't just impact the dinosaurs either. It affected all types of animals and plants that were living in many environments, including the ocean, and it didn't happen slowly. It happened in a blink of an eye (geologically speaking). Paleontologists have a special name for these events. They are called **mass extinctions.** The last mass extinction to hit the Earth occurred about 65 million years ago during the end of a geologic time period called the Cretaceous. This is when the dinosaurs were wiped out. Today, most scientists believe that the demise of the dinosaurs was the result of a large asteroid hitting the planet. When this happened, Earth's climate changed so much that only a few living things could survive.

BIO | WALTER AND LUIS ALVAREZ ONE BIG IMPACT ON PALEONTOLOGY

Unraveling the reason for the dinosaurs' extinction reads like the plot of a detective novel. The story begins in 1977, with an American geologist named Walter Alvarez. While working in Italy, he discovered a thin layer of 65,000,000-year-old red clay that marked the boundary between the rocks of the Cretaceous period below and the Tertiary period above.

Walter showed the clay to his father, Luis, a Nobel Prize–winning physicist. Luis tested it and discovered that the clay was rich in an element called iridium. Iridium is fairly rare on Earth but it is commonly found in meteorites.

Putting the pieces together, Walter suggested that the mass extinction at the end of the Cretaceous period was due to a large asteroid hitting the Earth. The impact would have thrown a huge amount of dust into the atmosphere, blocking out the sunlight and causing a sudden catastrophic climate change. The dust would eventually settle, forming the iridium-rich clay layer.

The biggest problem with the theory was that such a large asteroid should have made one really big crater—which no one had seen. That's because the crater was buried beneath several hundred feet of sediments underneath the waters of the Gulf of Mexico! Now most geologists support Alvarez's theory.

SOME PALEONTOLOGISTS HAVE SUGGESTED THAT NOT ALL THE DINOSAURS BECAME EXTINCT AT THE END OF **THE CRETACEOUS PERIOD.** THEY ARGUE THAT THE DINOS EVOLVED TO BECOME **BIRDS.** WHILE DINOSAURS AND BIRDS ARE CLEARLY RELATED, MOST PALEON-TOLOGISTS TREAT THEM **AS TWO DIFFERENT** AND DISTINCT ANIMAL GROUPS. THIS MAY CHANGE SOMETIME IN THE FUTURE AS NEW FACTS ARE DISCOVERED, BUT FOR NOW, WE CAN CONSIDER THE **DINOSAURS EXTINCT.**

THAT'S ONE STRANGE-LOOKING BIRD.

HERE'S WHAT IT MAY HAVE LOOKED LIKE AT THE VERY END OF THE CRETACEOUS PERIOD!

103

CHAPTER 9

THE DYNAMICS OF DIRT
SO MANY SOILS

A SOIL IS BORN!

You might not believe it, but dirt is pretty complicated stuff! The proper name for dirt is soil, and what makes soil special is its ability to grow plants. Soil, unlike a pile of sand, is something in which plants can grow. Most soils are a mixture of different things. Soil is mostly made up of mineral sediments, which come from the weathering of rock. Weathering is the process by which rocks are broken down into sediments. Most soils contain a mix of sediment sizes, including sand, silt, and clay. Some soils can also include gravel and large stones. You can see how a soil stacks up by doing the experiment below.

Organic muck soils can form in wet areas where there are lots of plants growing.

When you do the soil sorting experiment, you will probably notice stuff floating on top of the water. This material is called organic matter. It is really important to have organic matter in soil because it adds many important nutrients. Nutrients are the chemicals that plants need to grow. Organic matter can come from many sources, including rotten leaves, dead flowers, and the occasional dead animal. One of the most important sources of organic matter is animal poop!

So maybe you like your soil slimy? Some soil can be made up of mostly organic matter and have only a small amount of minerals in it. These organic-rich soils are called muck soils. Muck soils are usually found in wet areas such as swamps, marshes, and bogs. In these areas, the remains of plants in the water slowly build up and decompose. You know that you've found a muck soil when you step in the marsh and you immediately sink in with that telltale squish!

TRY THIS! 🧪 SORTING OUT SOILS

WHAT YOU'LL NEED

A cup of good old-fashioned soil from a garden or forest
A clear plastic 1-liter bottle with cap

A funnel
Water

WHAT YOU'LL DO

Fill the bottle three-quarters full of clean tap water. Use the funnel to carefully add the soil to the bottle so it begins to mix with the water. Screw the cap on the bottle so that it is tight and then shake the bottle hard for about ten seconds. Place the bottle on a table and watch what happens.

The sediment will begin to settle to the bottom. Allow the bottle to sit for about ten minutes and

observe it again. There should be several distinct layers of sediment of different sizes in the bottle.

When sediment is placed in water, the largest, heaviest particles settle first. These are followed by the smaller particles. When all the particles settle, you will see layers of the different-size sediments that make up the soil. Soil scientists use a similar technique when they analyze soils.

SOIL TEXTURE TRIANGLE

THE SOIL TEXTURE TRIANGLE IS A TOOL USED BY SCIENTISTS TO NAME
A SOIL BASED ON THE AMOUNTS OF SAND, SILT, AND CLAY FOUND IN IT.

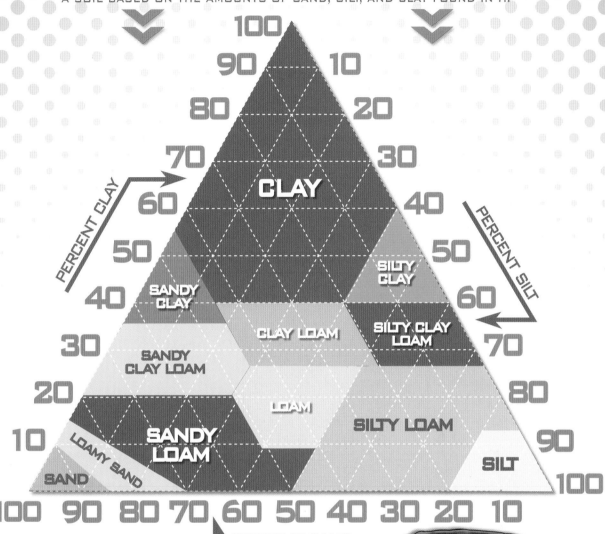

PERCENT CLAY

PERCENT SILT

100 90 80 70 60 50 40 30 20 10
PERCENT SAND

100 90 80 70 60 50 40 30 20 10

CLAY

SANDY CLAY

SILTY CLAY

CLAY LOAM

SILTY CLAY LOAM

SANDY CLAY LOAM

LOAM

SANDY LOAM

SILTY LOAM

LOAMY SAND

SAND

SILT

DIRTMEISTER'S NUGGET

MUCK SOILS CAN ACTUALLY BE **DANGEROUS** BECAUSE THE MORE YOU STRUGGLE TO GET OUT, THE **DEEPER YOU SINK IN!** YOU'LL NEED SOMEONE ELSE STANDING ON SOLID GROUND TO **HELP YOU GET OUT.**

HANG ON, DIGGER...I'LL PULL YOU OUT!

PROFILING SOILS

Just like you and me, soils take time to develop and mature. All soils begin with some sort of parent material. Parent material is the stuff that breaks down to make the soil. Some soils are made directly from solid rock. These take a long time to form because the rock has to weather in place. It is much more common for a soil to form from some type of sediment that has been carried into the area by wind, water, or ice. These soils usually form faster because the sediment is pre-weathered.

If you dig down through a soil you'll see that most are made up of several layers. Soil scientists call these different layers soil horizons. Mature soils tend to have more horizons than younger soils that are just starting to form. At the very top of the soil there is usually a layer of humus. Humus is another name for decomposed organic matter and it is usually dark brown in color. This layer is also pretty loose and fluffy.

The layer directly below the humus layer is the topsoil. The topsoil is the layer that plants sink their roots in to get nutrients and water. Old forest soils tend to have very thick topsoil and so do those that form below grasslands such as prairies.

If a soil has enough time to develop it will have another layer in between the parent material and the topsoil. This is called the subsoil, which is usually much harder to dig in than the topsoil. Quite often the subsoil is red, yellow, or orange. These colors come from chemicals that have been deposited in the soil by water flowing down through the soil from the topsoil above.

SOIL LAYERS

- HUMUS – O HORIZON
- TOPSOIL – A HORIZON
- SUBSOIL – B HORIZON
- PARENT MATERIAL – C HORIZON
- UNWEATHERED ROCK – R HORIZON

BIO EUGENE WOLDEMAR HILGARD FATHER OF AMERICAN SOIL SCIENCE

BIRTHPLACE: GERMANY   BIRTH YEAR: 1833

One of the first people to make the connection between climate and soil was a geologist named E. W. Hilgard. In 1853, Hilgard began doing chemical analysis of soils. He realized that much of what happens in the soil depends on factors such as rainfall and temperature. For the next 40 years he studied and taught about soils at several different universities. In 1892 he wrote a groundbreaking paper on the relationship between climate and soil and today is considered to be one of the founding fathers of American soil science.

GLOBAL SOIL MAP

BASED ON THE WORK OF E. W. HILGARD, SOIL SCIENTISTS TODAY CLASSIFY SOILS INTO DIFFERENT GROUPS DEPENDING ON THE CLIMATE AND PARENT MATERIAL THAT THE SOIL FORMED IN.

EACH COLOR REPRESENTS A DIFFERENT TYPE OF SOIL.

WOW! A LITTLE WATER SURE MAKES A BIG DIFFERENCE!

DIRTMEISTER'S NUGGET

CLIMATE IS ONE OF THE MOST IMPORTANT FACTORS IN DETERMINING THE TYPE OF SOIL THAT WILL DEVELOP. TWO AREAS CAN HAVE THE EXACT SAME PARENT MATERIAL, BUT IF ONE PLACE IS NORMALLY WARM AND HUMID AND THE OTHER IS COOL AND DRY, THEN THE SOILS THAT FORM IN EACH AREA WILL BE VERY DIFFERENT FROM EACH OTHER.

LIFE IN THE DIRT
THE SOIL ECOSYSTEM

While most people don't like having dirty houses, a lot of living things live in the dirt. In fact, one cubic foot (0.3 m³) of forest soil can have tens of millions of living things in it. Here are some living things you might find in the soil:

First and foremost, there are plants, the roots of which grow through the soil in search of water and nutrients. Along with plants, we also have fungi like mushrooms that live off of the dead organic matter. Then there are a whole host of large animals like moles, voles, rabbits, gophers, and, of course, prairie dogs like my pal, Digger! Next come all the smaller animals, including insects, millipedes, arachnids like spiders and mites, and everybody's favorite, earthworms! But why stop at the things you can see? The soil is also packed full of microbes. A microbe is a microorganism that is so small you need

Microbes are living things found in the soil that are so small you need a microscope to see them.

a microscope to see it.

All of the different life-forms found in a soil work together to create a complex web of life called a soil ecosystem. In an ecosystem, different living things have different jobs, but in the end they are all connected and depend on each other. One of the most important jobs in a soil ecosystem is done by the decomposers. Decomposers are nature's recyclers. They break down or decompose dead organic matter and animal waste products and release the nutrients back into the soil. Some of the most important decomposers are microscopic bacteria. Decomposers can also be larger life-forms, such as mushrooms that grow on dead wood, or insects, such as termites that eat the dead wood. If decomposers didn't do their thing, a soil would eventually run out of nutrients. In addition, instead of rotting away, the soil would just keep piling up with the bodies of old dead things!

MOLES HAVE POWERFUL FRONT PAWS THAT THEY USE FOR DIGGING THROUGH THE SOIL.

PRAIRIE DOGS BUILD MASSIVE TUNNEL SYSTEMS IN THE SOIL.

MANY TYPES OF ANTS BUILD COMPLEX COLONIES IN THE SOIL.

MUSHROOMS GET THEIR NUTRIENTS FROM DEAD AND DYING ORGANIC MATTER.

EARTHWORM POOP HELPS YOU! SOME OF THE MOST IMPORTANT DECOMPOSERS THAT ARE FOUND IN THE **SOIL ARE EARTHWORMS.** AS THEY **DIG** THROUGH THE **DIRT,** THEY SWALLOW FINE SOIL PARTICLES THAT ARE COVERED WITH ORGANIC MATTER. AFTER THEY **DIGEST THE GOOD STUFF,** THE WORMS **POOP** OUT TINY LITTLE BALLS OF DIRT CALLED **CASTINGS** THAT ARE CHOCK-FULL OF NUTRIENTS FOR PLANTS TO USE.

OK, DIGGER! I THINK THE SOIL HAS ENOUGH WORMS NOW!

PLANTING THE GOOD EARTH

Have you thanked the dirt today? You should! After all, if it were not for the soil, life as we know it would not be possible! Soil is one of our most important resources because it gives plants something to grow in, and we need our little green friends to provide us with food and oxygen.

Over the years, people learned how to manage soils in order to grow better plants. One of the first steps was cultivation, which involved clearing away plants that they didn't want to grow (such as weeds). They also discovered that tilling the soil so that it was loose, instead of packed down, would allow plants to grow faster and develop stronger roots. Most of these early discoveries happened because of trial and error. By the early eighteenth century, a few people started looking at soil from a scientific standpoint. They started experimenting with their dirt.

When it comes to growing crops, cultivation and developing new methods of tilling the soil were only the first steps. People also discovered that adding certain things, such as dead fish or manure (animal poop, that is) made the plants grow faster and stronger. People didn't know it at the time, but all of these things release chemicals, which the plants need to grow. Today we call these chemicals nutrients.

These days, farmers can test the soil and find out which nutrients are missing. They can then use fertilizers with different mixtures of chemicals to help a variety of plants. By selecting a fertilizer with the correct blend of nutrients, farmers can grow crops that are more productive than if they used plain soil.

> Archaeologists believe that people have been farming for over 11,000 years.

BIO JETHRO TULL BREAKS NEW GROUND

BIRTHPLACE: ENGLAND   BIRTH YEAR: 1674

When most adults think about Jethro Tull, the first thing that usually comes to mind is the English rock band by that name. But 300 years ago, an English farmer by the same name was busy trying to figure out ways to improve a soil.

The original Jethro Tull was the son of a farmer. He studied politics and law, and after graduating college, he traveled around Europe studying farms. When he returned to England he bought a farm and began to experiment with more efficient ways of tilling the soil and planting seed. The first thing he did was to invent a horse-powered hoe, which he used to dig up and loosen the soil so that the plants could grow better. Then he invented a device called a seed drill, which he used to carefully place seeds in even rows. In 1731, Tull published his methods in a book, and within a few decades, many farmers were using his methods. Tull's ideas laid the groundwork for modern agriculture.

This seed drill was one of Jethro Tull's inventions.

Modern farming techniques allow farmers to grow many more plants in one place.

The blue pellets here are a chemical fertilizer that has plant nutrients in a concentrated form.

These days many farmers use tractors instead of horses to help till and cultivate the soil.

DIRTMEISTER'S NUGGET

THE USE OF **CHEMICAL FERTILIZERS** ISN'T ALWAYS A GOOD THING. CHEMICAL FERTILIZERS OFTEN BUILD UP IN A SOIL AND OVER TIME RUIN A SOIL'S ABILITY TO **GROW PLANTS.** ALSO, WATER RUNNING OFF OF FARMERS' FIELDS CAN WASH THE FERTILIZER INTO **STREAMS AND LAKES,** WHERE **IT CAN HARM FISH** AND OTHER ANIMALS. THIS HAS LED MANY FARMERS TO USE OLDER TECHNIQUES WITH NATURAL FERTILIZERS LIKE ANIMAL MANURE. THESE ORGANIC METHODS ADD NUTRIENTS TO THE SOIL AND HELP KEEP IT LOOSE AND PRODUCTIVE FOR MANY YEARS.

KEEP SHOVELING, DIGGER, THIS MANURE IS GREAT FOR THE SOIL!

S.O.S.—SAVE OUR SOILS

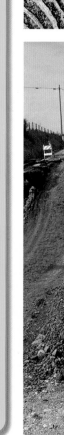

It's time for all Earthlings to come to the defense of the dirt! Since soil is such an important resource, it needs to be protected so that there will be enough of it to go around for future generations. Like air and water, soil can also be contaminated and polluted. By adding too many chemical fertilizers and using large quantities of pesticides to kill harmful insects and unwanted weeds, people can create soils that kill off many of the helpful life-forms found in a soil.

Another big problem is soil erosion, which happens whenever soil is washed or blown off the land. In a natural forest or prairie very little soil erosion occurs. This is because the soil is usually covered by grass or trees, and the plants on the surface help slow down soil erosion.

Unfortunately, for farmers to plant their crops, they have to till the soil, which means removing the old plants and digging up the top layer. This exposes the soil to the wind and rain, resulting in very serious soil erosion unless special measures are taken.

Of course, we can't blame farmers for all the problems with soil erosion because they are not the only ones digging in the dirt. Soil erosion can also be a big problem when people build new homes, roadways, or shopping malls. In some cases, soil loss from construction sites can be many times worse than it is on farmland.

When it comes to soil erosion, the loss of soil is only half the problem. This is where sedimentation comes into play. Once the dirt is removed from a construction site or farmer's field, it doesn't just disappear; it has to go someplace. It chokes streams or fills up lakes and ponds, ruining the habitat for the animals and plants that live there.

Sediment can also clog sewers or fill in reservoirs used for drinking water.

OK, so how do we solve the problem of soil erosion and sedimentation and save our soils? Well, fortunately, soil scientists have come up with a few cool ways to cut down on erosion. For example, instead of plowing straight up and down a hill, farmers can use something called contour strip cropping. This is when they plow around the hill, making it more difficult for water to erode the soil.

There have also been lots of improvements at construction sites. Instead of leaving soils bare, builders can cover them with mulch to help hold the dirt in place. They can also use barriers to trap sediment and protect drainage pipes.

Remember, it takes much longer for new soil to form than it does to lose it through erosion. As the Earth's population expands, and farmers have to grow more food, the need for good productive soil is only going to increase.

> Most people don't think of soil as a critical resource, but it is as important as clean air and water!

In many places, engineers use specially designed sediment barriers to help reduce soil erosion.

Terraces protect the soil from eroding.

Soil erosion is often a big problem along roadways in urban areas.

ONE OF THE LARGEST CAUSES OF SOIL EROSION IS THE IMPACT OF RAINDROPS. WHEN RAINDROPS HIT BARE SOIL THEY SPLASH SEDIMENT UP INTO THE AIR AND TURN IT INTO MUD, WHICH CAN THEN START TO FLOW DOWNHILL.

LOOK OUT, DIGGER, HERE COMES A MUDFLOW!

Modern farmers often use contour strip cropping to greatly reduce soil erosion.

115

ROCKY RESOURCES

For humans, rocks have really been a matter of life and death! Some of the very first tools that our ancient human ancestors depended on for their survival were made out of stone. Scientists believe that people began using stones for cracking open nuts and smashing animal bones around three million years ago. People also learned that rocks with a sharp edge could be used to cut up animals to eat.

Using naturally shaped stones as tools works fine, but you could waste a lot of time looking for a rock that had just the right edge on it. So they took matters into their own hands! Instead of hunting for the right-shaped rock, people started using rocks to shape other rocks, making their own custom-designed **stone tools!**

Early humans probably discovered how to make their own stone tools by trial and error and noticed that some rocks split in just the right way to make a sharp edge. You can try your hand at making your own stone tools by trying the experiment on page 119.

Our ancestors were very good at recognizing some of the useful properties of rocks. They found that hard minerals such as quartz and garnet were useful for smoothing and polishing softer stones. Softer rocks such as soapstone and marble were great for carving. In later years, some of the greatest artists in the history of the world, including Michelangelo and Leonardo da Vinci, would use marble to make incredibly detailed stone statues that have truly stood the test of time!

> Stone tools were often made of chert, a type of quartz that breaks with a sharp edge.

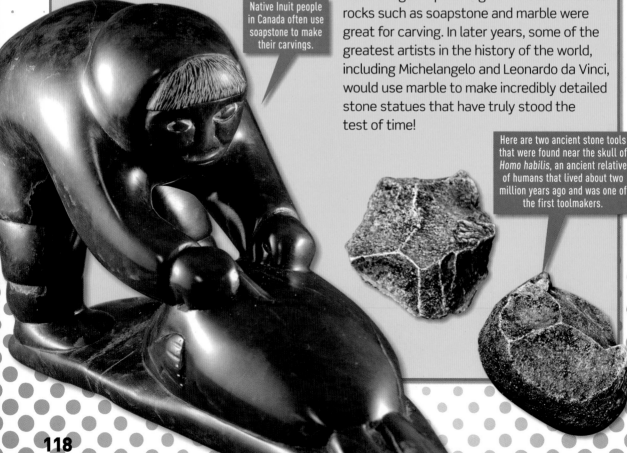

Native Inuit people in Canada often use soapstone to make their carvings.

Here are two ancient stone tools that were found near the skull of *Homo habilis*, an ancient relative of humans that lived about two million years ago and was one of the first toolmakers.

This famous sculpture, "Pietà" by Michelangelo, was carved from marble.

BACK IN THE EARLY 1960s, **ANTHROPOLOGISTS** LOUIS AND MARY LEAKEY MADE SOME INCREDIBLE DISCOVERIES OF THE REMAINS OF EARLY HUMANS IN A PLACE CALLED **OLDUVAI GORGE** IN TANZANIA IN EAST AFRICA. THE CREATURE THAT THEY FOUND WAS ABOUT **FOUR FEET TALL** AND SINCE IT CLEARLY USED TOOLS THEY NAMED IT *HOMO HABILIS*, WHICH IS LATIN FOR **"HANDY MAN."**

WOW, DIGGER, I WONDER IF THIS GUY KNOWS HOW TO FIX THE DIRTMOBILE.

HOMO HABILIS

TRY IT! 🧪 CHIPPING AWAY

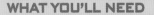

WHAT YOU'LL NEED

2 or 3 round stones, each about the size of your fist
Heavy work gloves
Safety glasses or goggles

WHAT YOU'LL DO

Warning: Before doing this experiment make certain that you are wearing heavy work gloves and eye protection! Start by holding one of the stones in your less dominant hand. So if you are right-handed, hold it in your left hand. This first rock is called the core and it is the one that will eventually be turned into your tool. Take the second rock in your dominant hand and gently tap it against the first at an angle. DO NOT SMASH THE ROCKS TOGETHER WITH A GREAT DEAL OF FORCE! Also, make sure you don't hit your fingers! Keep tapping on the core until you break off some small chips. Then rotate the core around to the outsideand repeat the tapping. After a few minutes you should wind up with a rock that has a wedge-shaped edge. Congratulations! You have made a hand ax! Much of the success of your toolmaking experiment will depend on the type of rocks that you have selected. Early humans discovered that not all rocks break the same. In order to get a sharp edge, you need a rock that is relatively hard and that fractures. Many of the best stone tools are made from quartz, flint, and obsidian.

Get an adult to help you out with this one!

119

STACKING STONES

Have you ever dreamed about designing really big buildings? It turns out that some of our early ancestors felt the same way! Somewhere around 7,000 years ago, people started **building cities.** Of course, there's nothing better than stone if you want to build a temple or palace that going to last for a while!

Building large structures with stone isn't the easiest thing to do. Large stones are very heavy and they are hard to shape. So instead of using rocks to build with, people used clay and mud to make bricks.

Making a **mud brick** is pretty easy. First, you build a frame out of wood to act as a mold. Then you mix clay soil with straw and add water to make a thick soupy mix, which is poured into the mold. The mold can dry in the sun and when it is removed, you have a brick!

Structures made from mud bricks work fine in dry places where it does not rain much. But when the bricks get wet, they begin to fall apart and turn back into mud. Instead of drying the bricks in the sun, people began baking them in ovens just as they did with pottery. This made the bricks much stronger and longer-lasting.

Of course, when it came to building very large structures, people had to use **stone.** When it came to stacking stones, nobody did it better than the ancient Egyptians, especially with those pyramids.

While the Egyptians were master pyramid builders, it was the ancient Greeks and Romans who took stone construction to whole new levels, building magnificent stone temples, roads, aqueducts, and even stadiums.

Today, people are still building with rocks. Modern buildings are often covered with decorative stone slabs, and stones are also used for paving walkways. In our homes, stone is used for building fireplaces and is even used for making kitchen countertops.

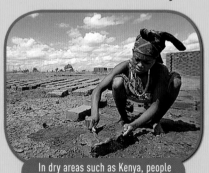
In dry areas such as Kenya, people still make mud bricks for building.

Since mud bricks fall apart after it rains they often have to be replaced.

The Egyptian pyramids were made mostly of limestone and granite.

CEMENT, WHICH WAS A ROMAN INVENTION, GETS ITS STRENGTH FROM A COMBINATION OF LIMESTONE, CLAY, AND GYPSUM THAT HAS BEEN GROUND UP AND HEATED **TO A HIGH TEMPERATURE.** WHEN MIXED WITH WATER AND **A BINDER SUCH AS QUARTZ** SAND, IT FORMS **A ROCK-HARD MATERIAL** AFTER IT DRIES.

WHOA, SORRY, DIGGER, I TOLD YOU NOT TO SNEAK UP BEHIND ME WHEN I'M MIXING CEMENT.

The Colosseum in Rome was one of the first buildings built with cement.

121

METAL MANIA

Are you into **heavy metal?** Not the music but things like lead, gold, and iron. Just about every piece of metal you see started as a rock. At first, people used metals found in their pure form as **nuggets.**

Both gold and copper can be found this way, so they were some of the earlier metals people worked with. Gold is so soft that it wasn't used much for making tools, but copper is hard enough to be turned into cutting devices like knives and simple saws.

A breakthrough came when people discovered that certain minerals had metals in them. The metals could be removed and concentrated when the rocks were crushed and heated. These metal-rich rocks are called **ores.** Just about every important metal, from aluminum to zinc, is removed from mineral ores mined from the ground.

Ores can be found in many rock types. Often, ores in igneous rocks form near large masses of granite. Some of the largest deposits of gold, silver, copper, zinc, and lead formed this way.

Not all metals start off as igneous rocks, though! In fact, most of the iron that is mined comes from rocks called **banded iron formations,** or BIFs for short. Most banded iron ores formed between 1.5 and 3 billion years ago, and they can be found all over the world. Geologists aren't sure how they formed—there are different theories about the process—but we do know that the process provided us an abundant resource.

> An ore is a rock that is mined for the metals that it contains.

BIO THOMAS EDISON MAGNETITE MINING MELTDOWN

BIRTHPLACE: UNITED STATES   BIRTH YEAR: 1847

Thomas Edison was successful at inventing many things, but one of his greatest failures was his plan to produce cheap iron and steel.

Back in the late 1800s, most of the iron ore in the United States came from banded iron formations near the Great Lakes. The ore was shipped to far-off mills to be turned into pure iron and steel. This made it very expensive.

Edison developed a plan to use powerful magnets to collect small pieces of magnetite ore from old iron mines and compress them into bricks. The bricks could then be sold to steel mills at a cheaper price than the ore from the Great Lakes.

Edison invented large magnetic separators and giant rock crushing machines to turn the magnetic sand into bricks. For ten years, he worked on this project, and while he was able to produce some iron, in the end Edison lost more than two million dollars! His dream of producing cheap steel turned into one big nightmare!

COPPER IS ONE OF THE FEW METALS THAT CAN BE FOUND AS A PURE NATIVE ELEMENT.

THIS COPPER SPEARHEAD IS FROM THE INDUS VALLEY IN ASIA.

IN THE 1920S, MINERS WORKED IN DANGEROUS CONDITIONS TO DIG ORE IN LEAD MINES LIKE THIS ONE IN MISSOURI.

FEELING FUELISH

Some rocks are just made to burn! Some of the most important natural resources that we get from the Earth are **fossil fuels,** including coal, oil (technically called **petroleum**), and natural gas. Fossil fuels are energy resources that power our modern world. Unfortunately, when fossil fuels are burned, they also put extra carbon dioxide into the atmosphere, which many scientists believe has caused the Earth's climate to warm.

Fossil fuels get their name from the fact that they were all formed from ancient life-forms (dead animals and plants). Since they are fossils, there is only a limited supply of them on planet Earth, and they will eventually run out.

Coal is a sedimentary rock that formed from plant materials that were buried in thick layers in a swampy environment where they couldn't rot. Instead, the dead plants piled up, eventually forming the coal we have today.

Some rocks have a bad case of **gas!** Both **petroleum** and **natural gas** are fluids that are contained inside of rock. How did that happen? Geologists believe that petroleum and natural gas came from tiny sea creatures that settled to the bottom after they died and eventually became mixed with sediment. Over time, heat and pressure "cooked" the dead critters, changing them into oil and natural gas. These fluids then became trapped in the spaces between the grains in the surrounding sedimentary rock.

> Fossil fuels are all formed from ancient life-forms.

BIO ISRAEL CHARLES WHITE Hits a Gusher

BIRTHPLACE: UNITED STATES   **BIRTH YEAR: 1848**

Israel Charles White loved his rocks! As a young boy he spent many hours collecting fossils and visiting coal mines near his family's home in West Virginia. After getting his degree, he joined the U.S. Geological Survey and soon became a leading expert on coal geology.

While White worked mainly with coal, he also became fascinated with petroleum. At that time the oil industry was just getting started and there was not a great deal of understanding of how petroleum moved and collected in rocks. Based on his work in coal, White was convinced that pools of oil would become trapped in folded rocks. He used his knowledge to discover a major oil field in West Virginia, which not only brought him much fame but made him a wealthy man, too!

For the next 30 years White taught college and spent much of his time traveling around the world looking for hidden oil deposits. His discoveries made the modern oil industry possible.

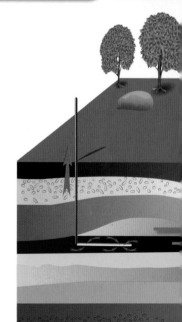

Today, most coal is mined by taking off the top of the mountain. This is also called strip-mining.

Coal is a sedimentary rock formed from the remains of ancient plants.

WELL THERE YOU HAVE IT, FRIENDS! THAT'S A SNAPSHOT OF OUR PLANET EARTH AND A LITTLE LOOK INTO WHAT MAKES IT TICK! AS FOR ME AND DIGGER, WE'RE OFF ON SOME OTHER ADVENTURES... MAYBE YOU CAN JOIN US, OR BETTER YET, HAVE SOME ADVENTURES OF YOUR OWN!

GAS
Natural gas collects at the top of the bend in the rock.

OIL
Crude oil flows up under the natural gas.

WATER
Since oil is less dense, it floats on the water below.

STEM SCIENCE STANDARDS

Each chapter in this book has been correlated with the Next Generation Science Standards (NGSS), which were developed by the National Research Council and are based on the Framework for K–12 Science Education. These standards describe important scientific ideas and practices that all students should learn and that should be incorporated with relevant science, technology, engineering, and math (STEM) concepts. The entries below identify each chapter in the book, outline its main ideas, and match those ideas with related NGSS life (L), physical (P), or Earth and space science (ESS) standards for grades 3–8. After each standard description, you'll notice a series of numbers and letters. These represent the grade level, subject area, and standard number. For example: 4-ESS1-1 translates into grade four, Earth and space science, standard number one. For more details on NGSS, **visit www.nextgenscience.org.**

HOW IT ALL BEGAN,
Pages 8-19
Understanding Earth's History
Identify evidence from patterns in rock formations and fossils in rock layers for changes in a landscape over time to support an explanation for changes in a landscape over time. (4-ESS1-1)

Construct a scientific explanation based on evidence from rock strata for how the geologic time scale is used to organize Earth's 4.6-billion-year-old history. (MS-ESS1-4)

MAGNIFICENT MINERALS,
Pages 20-31
Properties of Minerals
Make observations and measurements to identify materials based on their properties. (5-PS1-3)

EARTHQUAKES AND THEIR ORIGINS,
Pages 32-43
Earthquakes
Develop a model of waves to describe patterns in terms of amplitude and wavelength and show that waves can cause objects to move. (4-PS4-1)

Analyze and interpret data from maps to describe patterns of Earth's features. (4-ESS2-2)

Construct an explanation based on evidence for how geoscience processes have changed Earth's surface at varying time and spatial scales. (MS-ESS2-2)

FIRE DOWN BELOW,
Pages 44-55
Volcanoes
Analyze and interpret data from maps to describe patterns of Earth's features. (4-ESS2-2)

Construct an explanation based on evidence for how geoscience processes have changed Earth's surface at varying time and spatial scales. (MS-ESS2-2)

SHIFTING PLATES AND DRIFTING CONTINENTS, **Pages 56-67**
Plate Tectonics
Identify evidence from patterns in rock formations and fossils in rock layers for changes in a landscape over time to support an explanation for changes in a landscape over time. (4-ESS1-1)

Construct a scientific explanation based on evidence from rock strata for how the geologic time scale is used to organize Earth's 4.6-billion-year-old history. (MS-ESS1-4)

Analyze and interpret data on the distribution of fossils and rocks, continental shapes, and seafloor structures to provide evidence of the past plate motions. (MS-ESS2-3)

WHAT GOES UP MUST COME DOWN,
Pages 68-79
Weathering and Erosion
Make observations and/or measurements to provide evidence of the effects of weathering or the rate of erosion by water, ice, wind, or vegetation. (4-ESS2-1)

Construct an explanation based on evidence for how geoscience processes have changed Earth's surface at varying time and spatial scales. (MS-ESS2-2)

THE ROCK CYCLE,
Pages 80-91
The Rock Cycle
Identify evidence from patterns in rock formations and fossils in rock layers for changes in a landscape over time to support an explanation for changes in a landscape over time. (4-ESS1-1)

Develop a model to describe the cycling of Earth's materials and the flow of energy that drives this process. (MS-ESS2-1)

DIGGING OLD DEAD THINGS,
Pages 92-103
Fossils
Analyze and interpret data from fossils to provide evidence of the organisms and the environments in which they lived long ago. (3-LS4-1)

Analyze and interpret data for patterns in the fossil record that document the existence, diversity, extinction, and change of life-forms throughout the history of life on Earth under the assumption that natural laws operate today as in the past. (MS-LS4-1)

THE DYNAMICS OF DIRT,
Pages 104-115
Soil
Develop a model to describe the movement of matter among plants, animals, decomposers, and the environment. (5-LS2-1)

Develop a model to describe the cycling of matter and flow of energy among living and nonliving parts of an ecosystem. (MS-LS2-3)

ROCKIN' RESOURCES,
Pages 116-125
Natural Resources
Obtain and combine information to describe how energy and fuels are derived from natural resources and how their uses affect the environment. (4-ESS3-1)

Obtain and combine information about ways individual communities use science ideas to protect the Earth's resources and environment. (5-ESS3-1)

Construct a scientific explanation based on evidence for how the uneven distributions of Earth's mineral, energy, and groundwater resources are the result of past and current geoscience processes. (MS-ESS3-1)

Apply scientific principles to design a method for monitoring and minimizing the human impact on the environment. (MS-ESS3-3)

INDEX